SOCIAL SKILLS FOR TEENS

THE EMPOWERING HANDBOOK TO HELP YOUR KIDS
MAKE TRUE FRIENDS EVEN AS AN INTROVERT,
COMMUNICATE WHAT'S ON THEIR MIND, MANAGE
ANXIETY & HAVE THE CONFIDENCE TO SOCIALIZE

ALICE P.D. HANCOCK

CONTENTS

Teens And Social Anxiety　　　　　　　　　　　7

1. IT'S NICE TO HAVE A FRIEND　　　　　　13
Social Skills?　　　　　　　　　　　　　15
Why You Need Social Skills　　　　　　15
What Happens When You Have Poor Social
Skills?　　　　　　　　　　　　　　19
Can Social Skills Be Learned?　　　　　20
Verbal Skills　　　　　　　　　　　　22
Physical Skills　　　　　　　　　　　22
Thinking Skills　　　　　　　　　　　22
Social Skills Assessment　　　　　　　23
Action Steps　　　　　　　　　　　　26

2. TALK – WHY DON'T WE　　　　　　　　31
Why Is It So Hard To Talk
Shyness vs. Introversion vs. Social Anxiety　33
Fear Of Talking　　　　　　　　　　　39
Low Self-Esteem　　　　　　　　　　41
Social Anxiety　　　　　　　　　　　42
Activity - Positive Affirmation Day　　44
It Is Manageable　　　　　　　　　　44
Action Steps　　　　　　　　　　　　45

3. LET'S GET YOU TALKING　　　　　　　51
Simple Tips To Make Conversation
Why You Need to Talk　　　　　　　　52
Why Are Conversations Important?　　54
Listening is Communicating　　　　　56
What Exactly is Active Listening?　　　56
Active Learning Activity　　　　　　　61
Not Talking is Also Communication　　63
What is Non-Verbal Communication?　63
The Tea on Body Language　　　　　　65

Mastering Small Talks And Conversation 67
Action Steps 69

4. IT'S TIME TO MAKE FRIENDS 73
Friendship Skills 74
FORD Method 79
Frenemies & Toxic Friendships 82
When Someone Doesn't Want to be Friends 83
Action Steps 84

5. TOGETHER EVERYONE ACHIEVES MORE -
T.E.A.M. 89
Importance of Teamwork
Teamwork 90
Five Techniques For Effective Teamwork 92
What Makes A Successful Team 95
Collaboration Skills 96
Negotiation Skills 97
Action Steps 102

6. ALL IS BIG UNTIL IT IS SOLVED TO
BECOME SMALL 105
No Problems, Just Solutions
Problem-Solving Skills 106
Critical Thinking 108
Creative Thinking 109
Five Steps Of Problem-Solving 111
Resolving Conflict 113
Five Steps Of Conflict Resolution 115
Signs It's Bullying 116
Effective Communication 117
Activities To Do 119
Action Steps 121

7. DODGING THE EMOTIONAL TRAP 127
Managing Emotions and Feelings
Thoughts 130
Five Techniques To Regulate Your Thoughts 130
Emotions And Then Some 134
Emotional Regulation 135

Empathy and Compassion   139
Activity Time   140
Action Steps   141

8. THE PARENT CONNECTION CAN HELP
   YOU BE THE PERSON YOU WANT TO BE   145
Social Competence   147
Helping Them Decode Nonverbal Cues   150
Emotional Regulation   151
Teamwork   154
Action Steps   155

How It All Started   161
References   167

TEENS AND SOCIAL ANXIETY

Every day is a challenge. Mornings are the hardest. I always get to school early. The idea of arriving late and having everyone stare at me makes me sick to my stomach. Being early has its own issues but I get through it. I try to keep my head down so I don't have to say 'hi' to people I might bump into. I try to appear calm but there are days when it doesn't work and I find myself chatting in really fast, long-winded sentences with a sense of urgency. The reply I usually get is, "Just calm down" and "It will be okay" because I suspect no one wants that level of energy and worry early in the morning.

I feel a lot safer when I get to class but it only lasts till the teacher shows up. Wait? Did she say, Ryan or Ian? Is that my name she just called? Did she ask me a question? I quickly scan the room and spot Ian who is getting up to answer the question. Relief.

Have you ever had thoughts like these? Are you one of those who feel alone even when in a room full of people? Do you actively think of ways to not be in the spotlight? The thought of being the center of everyone's attention makes your palms sweaty. Does any of this sound familiar? Read on.

The trick is to look attentive but not too attentive. I reposition myself in the chair many times. I tinker with the pen. I doodle in the margin of the book as I copy everything the teacher writes on the board. All of a sudden, the pen falls. It rolls off the desk. I cannot get up. Everybody must be staring at me. My hands are shaking. Now my legs are shaking. I feel dizzy. My whole body is shaking, so much that my desk starts shaking too. I pick up my pen and continue drawing little vines. It's all I can do to distract myself.

The end of class means I can take a deep breath but the nauseating bewilderment returns as soon as I enter the crowded hallways where everyone has this laidback pace. I have lunch and 3 more classes to go. Should I go home? Should I say hello to one of the boys from my gym class? The girl from my science project waved at me during lunch. Should I sit with her or return to the bathroom for 139 more minutes? Should I do this? Should I do that?

Have you ever dealt with negative self-talk? Do you like being quiet or is it something you feel compelled to do because the alternative is scarier?

I hate myself. Why am I like this? I enjoy having conversations with my family members. I don't stop talking to them. Why is it so tricky with people in school? It wasn't always like that. I had friends in middle school. I participated in activities. Why am I so conscious of everything now?

Ryan is not alone in this predicament. You are not alone in this predicament. If you are reading this book, you have probably struggled with one of these scenarios at some point or another. Probably multiple times, if I am being honest.

Are you embarrassed to admit this? Don't be. It happens to many many of us, myself included. The world is filled with people like you and me, the kind who felt awkward, embarrassed, and downright incompetent every time they step out of the house. According to The National Institute Of Mental Health, social anxiety disorder (SAD) Over 19 million people across America suffer from social anxiety. Worth mentioning here is that it is quite intense in teenagers as well. It affects 1 out of 3 adolescents between 13 and 18 years old. It is the most common anxiety disorder and the third most common mental health disorder in the country. You are not alone.

If any of these scenarios describe you, I would say you are in the right place and doing the right thing. Anxiety, discomfort in social settings, and making friends or conversations with people intimidate or unnerve you. Physical reactions, such as headaches or stomachaches without a medical explanation, emotional reactions, such as crying or becoming overly upset over insignificant matters, thought reactions, such as worrying excessively without cause, and behavioral reactions, such as acting out beyond what you might expect from a situation, are some common signs of anxiety. These reactions are normal usually and can even be a result of stress, hunger, or a lack of sleep. But if they are continual and do not get better over time, you need to make some changes.

One of the first things that you need to do as you turn the pages of this book is to accept and understand that you have some form of social anxiety. It is not about putting yourself in a box but rather gaining an understanding of what it is that needs to be changed. Where did Ryan fit? Where do you fit? What do you do now that you know where you stand on the chart?

This may not seem like good news but there is some after all. Anxiety is not a disease that you set out to cure. It is not contagious that you need to hide. Instead, anxiety is a condition that can be managed. You just need to be willing to learn ways to cope. If you had a cut on your hand, you would put a band-aid. If you fractured your arm, you would visit the doctor.

Likewise, anxiety, depending on how intense it is, requires care. As you read through the chapters, the only request I would like to make is to keep an open mind and be willing to try out the ideas and suggestions mentioned here. Some will be easy, some will put you out of your comfort zone while some will straight up make you feel like they are impossible. When that thought hits you, take a deep breath, pause for a bit, and then return to the words you find here.

This book has many facets and while some may seem like your story, some might not. But there is something in it for everyone. I have included practical exercises and easy-to-do activities that you can practice on your own. Techniques to get along with people, techniques to utilize when you don't get along with certain people, how to get talking, ideas for small talk, problem-solving, conflict resolution, and managing your inner thoughts and emotions, you will find it all here. I have also added a self-assessment quiz to help you identify areas where you could use support. The action steps at the end of every chapter are a sure-shot way to practice the suggestions you can put into action, right away.

Use the experiences of others, their struggles, and weak moments, to navigate the pitfalls better. The cliche, knowledge is power really comes into play here and that's what I want to do - share my knowledge with you so you do not have to shrink yourself. Remember the discomfort you felt when you were in the spotlight or the worries of being called out by the teacher? Well if it's going to be uncomfortable anyway, let's aim for discomfort that will eventually make things better!

1

IT'S NICE TO HAVE A FRIEND

"In middle school and junior high, all my friends ditched me, so I was really lonely".

— TAYLOR SWIFT

Y*ou won't believe who said these words because you are so used to seeing her go up on stage and give performances that have millions dancing. She exudes confidence in every facet of her job and has at least twenty-one awards to her name. She is the first and only solo female artist to win the GRAMMY for Album Of The Year thrice. Yup Taylor Swift it is!*

Taylor Swift may seem to have it all now but she hasn't had an easy ride. Her social struggles may not be well known but they are well documented if you dig deep. Swift acknowledges that she never did well in school socially and expected to be more popular after becoming famous, but she feels as though she has fewer friends now than she did before. In one of her interviews, she said "I feel like I'm less popular than I've ever been. My best friend is Abigail and we've been friends since I was 15."

Things did not get better after finding fame either. She has had her fair share of hate in the public eye since she was young. Sometimes she was 'too annoying' or 'too skinny' or 'too petty, or 'too confident' and even a 'snake'. There was a lot of pressure to be a"good girl" which meant quietly toeing the line. There wasn't much choice but to keep up appearances and be the person everyone wanted her to be. The fear of never being enough drove her to the point where she would starve herself and experience dizziness when performing live.

She described relationships as fragile and tentative. She even disappeared for a long time because that's what she thought would make things better. In one of her interviews, Taylor says, "It can feel, at times, if you let your anxiety get the better of you like everybody's waiting for you to really mess up — and then you'll be done."

Taylor has come a long way and it wasn't without hard work. She focussed on her mental and physical health and in addition to making lifestyle changes, she started communicating with her mother regularly. She describes the journey as tough where she had to "destroy an entire belief system". She may not have a list of best friends but has managed to cultivate enough friendships to make life easy.

As I marvel at her courage to speak openly about her mental health struggles, let's acknowledge the fact that you can have record-breaking albums, a lavish lifestyle, access to the most fashionable of clothes, and invites to A-list parties and yet find yourself all alone in a corner. Whether you are famous and on stage or just living your own life, no one is immune.

SOCIAL SKILLS?

Social skills are important to help you navigate social situations. You need them to make friends, interact with teachers, and to even make a trip to the grocery store. You might be surprised to learn that there are many social skills that you use every day without realizing it. If you are curious to find out more about what the term "social skills" means, here is a breakdown.

WHY YOU NEED SOCIAL SKILLS

Social skills are the skills you use to communicate and interact with the people around you. They are tools that help you form a connection. By controlling your words, expressions, and actions, you can let the other person know what you want, or how you are feeling. Social skills help you get along better with your peers and other adults. They are not only limited to how you speak but include non-verbal communication, such as your gestures and body language. They also allow you to interpret what the other person is trying to communicate to you.

You use social skills whenever you engage with someone. You need social skills to do just about everything, from sending a text message (can you imagine reacting with the wrong emoji!) to ordering a latte. When you smile at the girl in class, when you say hello to the lady who works at Starbucks, when you look at your watch and sigh impatiently while waiting in line at the store, when you hold back a mean comment on someone's hair color are all instances of using social skills.

Social skills can be broken down into three parts; understanding feelings, both yours and the other person's, understanding the situation, and lastly, carrying out the right social behavior.

For instance, if you see someone crying in the school bathroom, your empathy makes you stop and realize that they might be sad and may need someone to comfort them. Your understanding of the social situation lets you judge if you know them well enough to comfort them, and how they might react if you asked what is bothering them. The right social behavior would be offering them a hug or a tissue to wipe their tears. Someone who does not have adequate social skills might ignore the situation completely.

There are no hard-and-fast rules for interpersonal skills. They are flexible and depend on the situation and the cultural setting. Here are a few benefits of developing good social skills.

Making Friends

Improving your people skills helps you build close friend-ships. It also makes you more confident and allows you to approach new people, making you less lonely. Well-honed social skills can make you sound interesting, and help give people the signal that you are warm and welcoming. For instance, sitting with your arms crossed and staring at the floor will make it less likely for someone to say "Hi!" to you in class.

Better Communication

Good communication skills are essential for being successful in life. Being able to speak clearly, nodding and shaking one's head and using appropriate hand gestures in conversation, expressing your opinion politely, making eye contact while talking, and learning to control your tone are all important aspects that help you become better at communicating. Good communication skills also make you more aware of what the other person is saying. They also make it easier for you to avoid people you do not want to spend time with. For instance, picture this. You're at a party and see Nick from your algebra class there. You dislike Nick and do not want to spend half your time making small talk with him. Having a good set of communication skills will help you politely give him the message and will give you more time to talk to other people.

Better Academic Performance

Children who are better adjusted socially find it easier to excel in academics. They have fewer disruptive behaviors which leaves them with more time and energy to focus on their studies. They also find it easier to approach their peers and their teachers for help.

Being Happier

People with good social skills are generally happier. They find it easier to approach more people and to make more friends, hence creating a strong support system for themselves. This boosts their self-esteem as well.

More Career Prospects

Most employers look for individuals with good people skills: They want you to work well in a team, and to motivate people to get work done. If you are not a good team player, chances are you will not get hired or promoted. Being socially skilled can help you perform better, especially if you are an entrepreneur or a sales executive. It helps you convince other people of your product's worth.

Being socially adept has other benefits too. Research shows that children who are socially adjusted are more likely to attain a high school diploma and continue their education after high school. They are also fewer chances of them falling into substance abuse, and they are less likely to break the law.

WHAT HAPPENS WHEN YOU HAVE POOR SOCIAL SKILLS?

Social skills are as necessary for a child's development as other skills, such as learning to read or write, ride a bike or eat with a spoon. They are an integral part of your ability to form meaningful and trusting relationships at home, in school or college, or later on in life. The trouble with these skills makes it difficult for you to succeed academically and socially.

Kevin was a 14-year-old and had just transferred to a new middle school. He had always been on the quieter side and was anxious about making friends. During lunch, he would sit alone and eat his food quietly. Occasionally, he would try to join a conversation but struggled to come up with something to say. Often he would want to share his thoughts on the latest series he was watching or talking about the latest TikTok trends, but he found himself falling silent. Over time he found himself feeling more and more lost, to the point that no one even noticed whenever he got up to leave. It always left him feeling upset and disappointed in himself. His grades started to slip, and he started skipping school frequently.

Like Kevin, if you are one of those who have trouble picking up on social cues, struggle to make conversation, or behave in a socially acceptable way, may find it hard to fit in. You may want to interact but cannot do it efficiently. When their interactions don't go well, you may feel detached This creates a vicious cycle of loneliness and isolation.

According to a new study from the University of Arizona, poor social skills may hurt physical and mental health. "People with poor social skills have high levels of stress and loneliness in their lives", said study author Chris Segrin, head of the UA Department of Communication. He explains this by using a simple analogy. The stress caused by loneliness can be compared to the way people feel when they are in a hurry to get out of the door but can't find their keys. The only difference is that with loneliness, the stress never goes away.

CAN SOCIAL SKILLS BE LEARNED?

Yes! Yes! Yes! The good news is that social skills can be learned, taught, and practiced. Just like you need to learn other skills, such as learning to drive or tie your shoelaces, you can learn appropriate social skills through practice, intentional effort, and guidance.

Parents are a child's first role models. They have the strongest influence on their child's life. Children pick up social cues and behaviors by observing their parents. When parents wait in line or respond calmly without yelling, they are teaching their children core social skills that will go a long way. If you find yourself struggling, reach out to your parents or any other trusted adult in your circle to get support.

Brad, a 15-year-old boy, had always been shy and introverted. He spent most of his time after school coding on his laptop. Not only did he struggle with making conversation face-to-face, but his parents also noticed that he avoided making eye contact with people, especially those he did not know well. He would often look down or away when someone tried to strike up a conversation. Anytime he had to look up in class, such as when he was asked to read aloud, he would start fumbling over his words.

Brad knew he had a problem and he felt embarrassed about it. Over the next weeks, with help from his parents, he started to work on maintaining eye contact. His parents encouraged him to hold eye contact for five to ten seconds at a time, before casually looking away for a few seconds. When Brad started to feel that people responded differently and showed more interest in what he was saying when he held their gaze he became more confident and made it a habit. There were times he still struggled, but he was no longer as awkward.

The first step towards practicing good social skills is to identify what sort of social skills you are struggling with. Social skills can broadly be classified into three different areas.

VERBAL SKILLS

These involve taking turns in conversation, not straining from topics in conversation, sharing appropriate information, paying attention to your tone of voice, accepting compliments graciously and returning compliments, not avoiding social situations that make you uncomfortable, making good introductions, and addressing people properly (That's right, you can't address your college professor as Bruh or Dude!).

PHYSICAL SKILLS

Making eye contact, respecting another person's personal space, and displaying correct body language and facial expressions are physical skills you must acquire to not be socially awkward.

THINKING SKILLS

These involve interpreting and responding to the other person's emotions and behaviors. Often, socially challenged children lack empathy and have trouble understanding someone else's perspectives and feelings; they cannot tell whether the other person is trying to be funny or sarcastic, and end up saying hurtful things. They cannot express their emotions in a socially acceptable way.

Acquiring social skills is a gradual process. Just like you cannot become a pro at algebra or learn the periodic table overnight, you cannot become socially savvy all of a sudden. It takes time and patience. It is important to remember that there is no one-size-fits-all approach to learning social skills. What works for one individual may not work for the other. But it is paramount that every child should be given opportunities and support that will enable them to become well-rounded and successful.

SOCIAL SKILLS ASSESSMENT

Wondering how socially competent are you? Do you have what it takes to engage people in meaningful conversation and forge good friendships? Can you socialize with anyone without feeling anxious or awkward? Take this social skills assessment and find out.

Questions Describe The Situation Put an X in the box that's best			
Communication Skills	**Often**	**Sometimes**	**Rarely**
I initiate conversations with other people			
I find it easy to start a conversation			
I make appropriate comments related to the topic being discussed at the right time			

I end conversations appropriately			
I maintain eye contact during a conversation			
I use non-verbal cues like nodding my head and hand gestures during a conversation			
I ask questions that show interest in what the other person is saying			
I feel comfortable speaking up in group discussions			
I listen attentively			
I handle awkward silences well			
I adjust my tone to match the situation i.e. I know when I need to speak formally and when I need to speak casually			
My tone is friendly and welcoming			
I talk about things that interest both of us			
I take turns in conversation and give the other person a chance to speak up			
I maintain appropriate proximity with the person I'm speaking to, neither getting too close nor stepping back			

Emotional Regulation and Empathy	Often	Sometimes	Rarely
I can identify and label my emotions			
I can identify and understand the emotions of others			
I am good at finding solutions to problems			
I do not become angry or upset when something does not turn out the way I want it to			
I do not resort to aggressive behavior			
I can handle disagreements amicably, without arguing or fighting			
I try to help people end arguments			
I let others know how I am feeling in a positive way			
I take a break or use another coping mechanism (e.g. deep breathing) when I'm feeling overwhelmed			
I consider the impact my actions have on other people			
I stand up for a friend who is treated unfairly			

I respond to other people's emotional needs, like cheering someone when they're sad and sharing their excitement when they're happy			
I try to understand the other person's point of view			
I offer the other person help with a task			
I accept unexpected circumstances positively			

If you find yourself ticking the "Often" option for most of the skills mentioned above, you are doing okay. . If most of your responses are either "Sometimes", you are halfway there and need to pay attention to what's shared in the forthcoming passages. For those of you who ticked "Rarely", help is always available. Read on, take small steps every day, and remember that it can and will change. There is some work ahead of you but it's manageable.

ACTION STEPS

If you are trying to become socially competent, here are some strategies you can use.

1. Find Out Your Problem Areas

To improve your social skills, you first need to identify which skills you are struggling with. Brad was able to carry on a conversation once he was spoken to, but he would never be able to initiate it, especially if he was surrounded by new people. He was unable to walk up to someone and introduce himself. It left him feeling left out and frustrated. Finding out his trouble areas made it easier for him to figure out the solution. His parents suggested striking up a conversation with the new girl on his school bus. Despite being nervous, he asked her how her weekend went.

The conversation flowed naturally from there. After the first few times of trying this approach, he became more confident and could easily walk up to anyone and say, "Hi! I think we're in French together. What did you think of the last assignment we got?" or "Have you tried the new chicken wrap that was served for lunch today. It was pretty good."

2. Learn Through Feedback

Asking a friend or a trusted adult to help you in improving your social skills can be a great way to become less awkward. Learning how you come across to the other person gives you a chance to work on yourself. However, remember to take criticism constructively and not get offended.

You could try saying something like, "You always seem to know what to say. Could you give me a few pointers on how I can improve my social skills?", "I am trying to be more friendly, but I am not sure how I am doing. Can you tell me if it's working?" or "Do you think I come across as very aggressive?"

3. Be Approachable And Welcoming

Everyone wants to connect with people who appear warm and friendly. Smiling is the easiest way to make people more comfortable in your presence. Making eye contact is also an essential social skill; it shows the other person that you are interested in what they're saying. It sounds easy but it makes some teenagers uncomfortable. If holding the other person's gaze makes you anxious, try the 50/70 rule. When you're talking, maintain eye contact 50 percent of the time and 70 percent of the time when you're listening. Pay attention to your body language. Sitting with your arms crossed or with a bored expression on your face doesn't make you look very friendly.

4. Set Goals For Yourself

Try to come up with a plan to improve your people skills. Set simple and specific goals that you can easily achieve. Remember to start small and gradually build up your plan. Examples of some goals that you can try are:

- Smile and make eye contact with at least 2 new people.
- Ask the bus driver how their day is going.
- Compliment someone. "I really like your jacket. The color looks great on you."
- Spend at least 15 minutes doing something out of your comfort zone.

- Keeping track of what you have achieved will keep you motivated.

5. Learn From Examples

Observe how people interact in social settings. Notice what social cues they use and pick up phrases that you hear. Pay attention to how socially skilled people handle disagreements, and how they show interest in others. Observing real-life social situations will give you a better understanding of how to use humor and sarcasm effectively.

6. Look For People With Common Interests

Getting involved in an after-school activity helps you connect with people you have something in common with. Join a club or try out for a sports team. Being part of a group of people working towards the same goal gives you a sense of social support. It also teaches you teamwork and improves your communication skills. Volunteering at local animal shelters and soup kitchens is also a good way to brush up on your social skills and gather empathy. Someone I was talking to the other day mentioned how her daughter started writing for the school newspaper. Though she was quiet and reserved, she was a gifted writer. Working as a team with the editors and illustrators and being on the ground to cover all the school events helped her overcome her shyness while doing something she enjoyed.

7. Explore New Cultures

Learning about what people have in common and embracing their differences can help you become more open and inclusive. Having conversations about different experiences can build a sense of empathy and help you see the world through a different cultural lens. Trying to communicate with someone who doesn't speak the same language as you can make you pay more attention to non-verbal communication, such as hand gestures and facial expressions.

Having well-developed social skills is a vital tool for success. It helps you deal with tricky social situations, build better connections with your peers, and form lifelong friendships. It improves your self-esteem and makes you a confident and empathetic individual. Social skills come naturally to some people while others may feel awkward or out of place in social situations. For these people, social interactions can be hard and intimidating. With the right guidance, anyone can overcome social anxiety and become a pro at socializing.

2

TALK – WHY DON'T WE

WHY IS IT SO HARD TO TALK

I *often hear my classmates complaining about their parents putting limits on the number of events and get-togethers they can attend. Almost everyone I know or seem to know has a long list of social events they have lined up. Yet, there wouldn't be much in my diary if I were to ever write one.*

I just turned 18 and even though I have the family car at my disposal, I really don't have many places to go to. It's not that I don't get invited to parties. I just decline the invites because being in a room full of people gives me anxiety.

I tried attending some because my friends insisted but I couldn't shake the feeling of panic that took over. I remember spending the better part of the night in the restroom because it felt like there were too many people in one place. I could barely breathe until I found solace in the backyard.

A bunch of people were already there. I tried to look for a corner where I wouldn't have to acknowledge anyone. As my friend recounted later, I was standing like a statue, staring into space. My friends tell me to loosen up and relax but I just cannot. I mean it's like being stuck between a rock and a hard place.

If I keep turning down invitations, I might stop getting invited and I don't want that to happen. That shouldn't bother me though because I like being on my own. But I also like having friends and being invited to places. What if my friends also quit on me? But every time there is a social event, I spend the week before worrying about how I will survive it.

Beth is a perfect example of anxiety on a loop. Her worries keep her up at night. Damned if you do, damned if you don't. She wanted to hang out with people but felt uncomfortable doing so. Some people are open to new things and people. They frequently initiate conversation and are the first to introduce themselves. They enjoy social interactions and will gladly wave at people they happen to know. On the other hand, some people are quiet and reserved and like to ease into unfamiliar settings or circumstances. They may join the party but find it difficult to dance or participate in the conversation. Was Beth shy? An introvert? Or someone with social anxiety?

Shyness is universal and affects enough people globally to warrant a study of its own. The American Academy of Pediatrics interviewed over 10,000 adolescents, aged 13 to 18 years, to figure out exactly this. As per the results, about

62% of parents reported that their adolescents were shy, whereas approximately 47% of adolescents thought that they were shy (Burstein, M. et al, 2011). The same study also notes that about 12% of adolescents interviewed had social anxiety (referred to as phobia).

SHYNESS VS. INTROVERSION VS. SOCIAL ANXIETY

Before putting yourself in a box, it is imperative to understand the different variations.

Shyness is how a person acts around other people. Feeling uneasy, conscious, anxious, nervous, unsure, or insecure can all be symptoms of shyness. Shy people can also have physical symptoms like blushing or being breathless, shaky, or silent.

Introverts, on the other hand, have no aversion to social situations. They simply prefer spending time with themselves and limit social interactions voluntarily. Shy people, on the other hand, want to interact with others but might be reluctant to because they don't want to draw attention to themselves or their awkwardness.

Yet, some people can experience excessive shyness. Known as Social Anxiety Disorder (SAD), the shyness develops into this powerful fear that disrupts their ability to function in social settings, attempt new things, or meet acquaintances (Usually new but also people they are familiar with). In addition to avoiding commonplace circumstances like talking to peers or teachers, people with acute SAD may also have trouble eating in public, speaking on the phone, placing a meal order, or using a public restroom. SAD is characterized by anxiety and self-criticism as well as the worry that others will judge their public performance. Introverts can manage, and shyness can be overcome over time but it is the SAD class of people that needs extra help.

When It's Not Just Shyness

Social skills are the skills we use every day to interact and communicate with others. They comprise both verbal and non-verbal cues such as gestures, body language, facial expressions, and speech. A person has high social skills if they are aware of how to act in social circumstances and comprehend both explicit and implicit social rules. Everyone experiences awkward moments but if you are struggling with conversations or constantly experiencing awkward silences, you might need a helping hand.

Let's face it, social skills are important even if it may not seem like it right now. They are crucial in making and sustaining friendships. For instance, you may be happy spending all your free time playing video games and it may not feel like a big issue but in a few years, you might realize that you need to develop people skills to find a girlfriend.

Lack of social skills can become problematic in many areas of life. You risk losing out on opportunities and activities, appearing out of step, or acting in a way that alienates people. You may have a hard time reading social cues and adhering to social norms. You may find it difficult to socialize, make friends, and collaborate with others.

There are numerous reasons why some people struggle with social skills. The cause may occasionally be temporary but may also stem from significant, lifelong difficulties. Several factors can affect how people interact with others. Some common ones include:

1. Lack of Experience

This is one of the most common reasons for poor social skills - you don't know how to interact with people because you haven't really done it much. This is especially relevant in the post-pandemic world where we were forced to minimize our interactions. We were stuck in our homes, without interacting with our neighbors, friends, and family. We were forced to shrink our pool of people and so many of us became comfortable with that way of life.

Like any skill, you need practice to hone it. Experience is essential. The more you talk, the better it gets.

2. Anxiety

Anxiety - the feeling of uneasiness - might just be the original cause. Some people approach the world with more restraint and inhibition than others. Simply said, the wiring in their neurological systems makes them more responsive or sensitive to stimuli. They usually resist change in their environment even as infants and toddlers. They take longer to 'warm up' to new situations. An anxious temperament is frequently linked to shyness which leads to avoiding social situations.

Moreover, people with anxiety typically find it difficult to express their thoughts, which makes conversations and encounters all the more difficult. They are apprehensive and avoid speaking up and taking part in group activities. "What if I say the wrong thing?" "What if everyone laughs at me?"

Even people with good social skills can feel anxiety and find themselves in awkward situations simply because they find it difficult to project confidence.

3. Environmental Factors

The family environment and experience in other social settings may lead to ineffective social relationships. Children who grow up in homes with a lot of conflict or tension may be less likely to acquire effective social skills. A child is more likely to experience difficulties in their own relationships if he sees his parents struggle with communication. The absence of positive role models may have detrimental effects. If you are typically a child in a house where you face criticism or teasing that is disguised as playful but in reality is hurtful, you risk seeing the world with the same lens. You fear the same reaction from the world at large as you experienced in the house, a place where you should ideally feel safe.

4. Social Media

The rise in communication via social media tools is also shaping how many of us approach social skills. People in your age bracket, (teenagers and adolescents) spend numerous hours on their smartphones interacting with their Instagram, Facebook, Snapchat, and Twitter accounts as well as texting and messaging friends. Social media notifications they receive during the day may have an impact on how they feel and think about themselves. This can be a fun and rewarding experience in some ways, but it can also increase anxiety, feelings of loneliness, and melancholy.

There is no denying that social media can support friendships and family connections for children and teenagers, but it can also encourage bullying and have a bad impact on self-esteem and self-image. It is very easy to say mean comments when you are hiding behind your screen. The number of likes you receive on your latest comment cannot serve as a testimony of your awesomeness. The lack thereof can make many feel uncomfortable. Social media success or failure is not an indicator of your social skills. It may seem like you are talking to a lot of people online, but nothing can replace the experience that comes from conversing with people in person. Emojis and emoticons are not the only way to express and convey emotions.

5. Past Failures or Trauma

A young girl may resist the urge to raise her hand in class because a teacher once got angry with her for a random reason. A boy may avoid trying for the basketball trials because his classmates laughed at him the last time he made a mistake. The new girl probably eats her lunch in a corner of the courtyard because she fears social rejection will follow her in the new school too.

Our experiences, traumas, and mistakes shape the way we approach and exhibit social skills in life. Bullying, being yelled at, or being in a situation that has left us scarred can significantly impact how we behave in social settings.

6. Underlying Conditions - ADHD/Depression

Due to their inattention, impulsivity, and hyperactivity, people with ADHD frequently struggle in social situations, feel rejected by others, and have relationship issues. Such unfavorable interpersonal consequences result in emotional sorrow and pain.

In the case of depression, a person can completely cut oneself off from everything and everyone, including their friends. Poor social skills may stem from some of them avoiding social situations because they don't want to burden others. They might not even know they are depressed. Some are in denial.

Mental health should never be taken lightly. Seek out expert advice if you think you are struggling.

One of the above-mentioned reasons probably resonates with you. Or it could be more than one. I know this doesn't make you feel better (yet) and it doesn't seem to solve any of your problems. There is a 'yet' after this statement too. No, knowing the cause or accepting that you have poor social skills is not going to make you feel lighter right away but when you go to bed at night, tell yourself that you are not alone. It affects many more. It is happening to so many around you. That there is help available and that you are not a statistic or the odd one out.

FEAR OF TALKING

Poor social skills usually manifest in difficulty in speaking. This is a physical issue where you feel that your mouth can't move properly or that your tongue is too wide, as well as a psychological issue where you're afraid of speaking in front of others. These signs and symptoms accompany various forms of anxiety.

Let's go over possible reasons why you may have trouble speaking.

- Fear of Being Judged: You are overly cautious, sensitive, and risk-averse. You feel like people think there is something wrong with you. "What is wrong with him?". "Why doesn't he have anyone to talk to?". One mental and emotional challenge that might make it challenging to speak comfortably in front of people is the fear of being criticized. The fear that others will look down on them if they speak is a common one and can deter many from talking.

- Overthinking: I am an analyst by profession now but I have been called one forever. I am an overthinker. I look at things from a hundred different angles before verifying them. No surprise that I analyzed and overanalyzed my communication with people too. There are many more me who spend too much time considering how to say something, how they are feeling, hows it will make the other person feel, and so on. The more they reflect on it, the more they struggle to form coherent sentences. What often happens is they lose track of the conversation, and then all of a sudden they realize that the time has passed and they are unable to continue.

- Rushing Thoughts: You are thinking a hundred things simultaneously and somehow when you say them out, the thoughts and the words leap from one to the next and people find it difficult to follow you. Rushing thoughts make it challenging to talk to since they make you feel stressed, overwhelmed, and unable to think out what you want to say and how you want to deliver it properly.

- Mouth Movements: Speaking is one of those bodily activities that can be difficult when you're feeling stressed. The stress and anxiety that comes with talking consume all your energy and you are left with a delayed reaction/coordination situation which makes it difficult for you to move your mouth's muscles. It happens to me often, especially in conversations where the words form in my head but never really leave my mouth.

LOW SELF-ESTEEM

Among other things, low self-esteem has an impact on social interactions. When you don't feel good about yourself, you could have crippling self-consciousness and fear that other people won't think highly of you either. Because of this, a lot of people with poor self-esteem may make an effort to avoid social situations, which might ultimately make their problems worse.

If you're someone who struggles with low self-esteem, you likely question and worry about everything you say and do before, during, and after a social interaction. Persistent self-criticism is your enemy. This can entail putting a critical lens on everything you say and do and overanalyzing it. You can start to feel as though your behavior is odd, embarrassing, or annoying. You loathe yourself and hence easily convince yourself that others feel that way too.

It's critical to keep in mind that no one is examining you as close as you are. Nobody is as concerned as you are. You would be shocked at how drastically other people's perceptions of you differ from your own. Being real is the key to overcoming self-criticism. This entails accepting the entirety of who you are, including all of your eccentricities and social ineptitude.

SOCIAL ANXIETY

Social anxiety is a constant fear that affects daily life, relationships, relationships with others, and life at work or in school. Although many people worry occasionally about social situations, people with social anxiety worry excessively before, during, and after them. You may have social anxiety if you:

- Avoid or worry a lot about social activities like group chats, and eating with people
- Worrying about everyday activities like meeting strangers, striking up conversations, talking on the phone, working, or shopping

- Always be concerned about doing something you think will make you look foolish, like blushing, perspiring, or being incompetent.
- Find it challenging to perform tasks when others are present
- Avoid eye contact, feel as though you are constantly being observed and scrutinized, fear criticism, or experience symptoms like nausea, shaking, sweating, or a racing heartbeat (palpitations)
- Experience panic episodes

Anxiety Begets Anxiety

Beth may believe she is dodging the bullet by skipping those parties or hiding in a corner but that's not true. By avoiding challenging your anxiety, you make it stronger. You feed the fear which is known as "negative reinforcement". Had she gotten up there and danced, she might have been less anxious the next time. The fact that she stood still intensified her initial feelings of worry and increased the likelihood that she would decline the challenge in the future.

It can be extremely unsettling to feel as though your muscles or your brain are malfunctioning and you are physically unable to speak or move. It can feel as though there must be something seriously wrong with you. The reality is, nothing is wrong; it is anxiety making you feel this way. Even if there is, you have no way of finding out till you actually test it. The more you avoid it, the bigger the demon it becomes. How to beat it? Take small steps. I have high-lighted a few action steps. Before we head there though, it is time for some positive affirmation for you.

ACTIVITY - POSITIVE AFFIRMATION DAY

Do this today. Ask a friend, a family member, a neighbor, or a sibling to sit with you for a moment and write something positive about you. Tell them to be honest and realistic and only mention something true. Do this exercise with 3-5 people. This is a great way to see yourself from the eyes of others and may allow you to hear your potential strengths.

Alternatively, develop a mantra or an affirmation that can help you get through a tough time. If you are struggling to think of one, here are some examples:

- It will be ok
- It will be okay even if it doesn't seem ok right now
- I got this
- Learning is an active process and I will learn by doing
- If it is to be, it's up to me

IT IS MANAGEABLE

You can do it. That is all I know and that is all I would say to anyone who has struggled because I said it to my daughter every time she came back disheartened. I repeated the same words when she took those steps to better up. Asking for assistance can be challenging, but a doctor will make an effort to make you feel at ease because they are aware that many individuals experience social anxiety. If you are comfortable, speak to your school counselor or ask a trusted adult to connect you with your General Practioner. They will likely ask you questions about your emotions, actions, and symptoms and will refer you to a specialized mental health professional to do a thorough evaluation and discuss available therapies.

ACTION STEPS

Try out the strategies listed below to get over social anxiety and gain confidence:

1. Look Confident

Project the image even if you don't feel it. Your body language mirrors your mental moods so a slouching posture indicates avoidance. Head up and you look confident without saying a word. You can deliberately use confident body language to feel more assured. Standing and sitting with good posture, slow movements, and raising your hands above your head can give them compression that you are confident, without doing any talking. There is science behind it too. Confident poses lower cortisol, the stress hormone, and increases the production of other neuro-transmitters, such as dopamine and serotonin, which are usually associated with feeling good. By projecting confidence through your body language, you can begin to believe that you can overcome your social anxiety.

2. It Is Okay To Be Awkward

Tell yourself that, several times. Everyone feels awkward, even the most confident-looking people. They might feel uncomfortable proposing a first date to a crush. The only difference is they go ahead and ask. They know that if they don't ask at all, they will never get that date. Feeling awkward is normal. Everyone messes up occasionally. everyone fears being awkward or uncomfortable but you don't let it stop you from following your desires.

3. Embarrass Yourself On Purpose

Meet your biggest fear. Set yourself up for the failure that you have been dreading all these days. Let people laugh at you. Set a day aside and consider intentionally embarrassing yourself, mildly. This is fairly easy to do in social situations. Think of wearing something a little out of the ordinary. Introduce yourself to someone you don't know. Go to a place where no one knows you and laugh loudly. This might be quite difficult for someone with severe social anxiety and yet, if you can get yourself to try these out, you will probably feel more at ease speaking in front of others.

4. Take Slow, Steady Steps Forward

You can move slowly as long as you are moving forward. Say hello to a classmate on day one. Acknowledge a teacher on day two. Create goals. You don't have to join the most popular table in the cafeteria, but you can sit at a table. Someone might join, today or tomorrow. Look up and smile at people passing by in the corridor. By excluding yourself from situations that can make you feel shy, you strengthen your shyness and keep it at a level that is difficult to overcome. Doing the opposite will help you gain confidence a little at a time.

5. Maintain A Record Of Your Interactions

Of course, you don't have to record each exchange but, keep track of the instances in which you had the chance to avoid a situation but chose to confront your fear and proceeded anyhow.

This will serve as a useful reminder of the strides you have made in overcoming your social anxiety and gaining confidence. Even a small amount of time can be used for this. The next time you come home from a social function, write down your impressions of one or two exchanges.

6. Nurture Your Existing Friendships

You may not know many people but there must be someone you consider a friend or have friendly terms with. Reach out to them, connect, try to find common ground, and do an activity together. Having friendships boost confidence, and the more you can change to get closer to individuals and practice speaking with them, the easier it will be to interact where other people.

7. Exercise

Although it may not seem like exercise has anything to do with speaking, there is a connection. Exercise causes your body to release neurotransmitters that elevate mood and make it easier to feel at ease conversing. Exercise also seems to boost self-confidence, which can have a significant impact on your capacity to connect with and form relationships with others. Start working out right away, and you could discover that speaking is a lot simpler. And while you are at it, smile and acknowledge the people you encounter as you jog around or hit the gym.

People like you and me avoid social interactions. We give ourselves fewer opportunities to practice social skills. The truth is, social skills get easier and seem more natural as you practice them more. You don't have to talk a lot to be socially comfortable - it is a subtle balance between talking and listening. The next chapter outlines how you can do both these and polish your communication skills.

3

LET'S GET YOU TALKING

SIMPLE TIPS TO MAKE CONVERSATION

N*ick was a High School junior who always kept to himself. He found it difficult to make conversation and had a hard time dealing with social situations. He often felt left out at school events; he usually ended up standing in a corner as everyone hung out and laughed together.*

When it was time for the school dance, Nick decided he will go and try to have a good time. He was excited, but the thought of having to engage with so many people made him very nervous. He felt overwhelmed and lost once he got there. Nick tried to make small talk but found himself struggling with what to say. His mind had gone completely blank.

Like Nick, if the thought of putting yourself out there makes you feel judged and makes conversations difficult, you are not alone. Most teens feel anxious when talking to others and this can make feel them feel isolated.

Many celebrities experience this too. Your favorite actor or singer may have been nervous about being around others at some point in their life. Celebs like Lorde and Alessia Cara have spoken up about being shy. Alessia Cara's song "Here" may be a hard relate for anyone who is struggling socially. It is all about hating being at a party and has become an anthem for introverts the world over. Lady Gaga has also spoken about being shy and insecure even though she is probably the last person you would imagine having confidence issues. She has spoken up about not wanting to "talk to anyone at the big celebrity functions."

Knowing that you are not the only one having a hard time can provide a sense of relief. Many people experience similar challenges while dealing with social situations. But don't stress about it. There's some seriously good stuff waiting at the end of the tunnel. With a little effort, you can legit learn to vibe with anyone. Just keep practicing and you'll slay the convo game.

WHY YOU NEED TO TALK

The ability to talk is vital for doing almost everything. It helps us communicate, build connections, and express ourselves. Have you ever wondered what would happen if you were unable to talk to anyone? How would you gossip about your latest crush, share about your favorite celeb noticing you on Tiktok, exchange notes on the new video game that everyone is raving about, or rant about the missed goal in the game last night? You wouldn't be able to bond with your friends or laugh over an inside joke. Talking has a lot of advantages, enough to make even the most introverted want to speak up more. Let me break it down for you.

Exchanging Stories

Talking about your problems can help take the weight off your shoulders. It can help you unwind and feel more in control of the situation. The next time something bothers you, find someone to talk to and let it all out.

Bond With Your Squad

Talking helps you bond with the people around you. It helps you build better connections and strengthens your friendship. Studies show that people who have good relationships with others are happier, healthier, and live longer. They are also less likely to be depressed.

Look from a New Angle

When you're feeling down, it can be tough to think of things from a new perspective. Talking to someone can help think of a solution from a fresh angle. Bouncing ideas off each other can introduce you to different viewpoints.

Talking Helps You Get Through Feelings

Talking to someone can give you the support you need to do anything. Knowing someone's got your back makes you feel less alone. Having a squad who listens to you without any drama can give you the space to be your true self.

WHY ARE CONVERSATIONS IMPORTANT?

Having a conversation is one of the most important things we can do as humans. It's a powerful way to build a connection. The main goal of talking to other people is to understand them better. When we converse, we share our thoughts and feelings. We listen to what others have to say and we try to understand where they're coming from. We zone in and out, pause between words and sentences, and try to fill it up with meaningful exchanges.

When we have a conversation, we listen, we build on what someone else said, we bounce ideas off each other, and we ask questions and give feedback. It helps us learn and think things through. TBH conversation isn't just words; it's creating a real connection with someone. It's hard to empathize when we don't have real convos.

What Makes a Conversation Work?

If you're wondering what makes a good conversation, here are the ingredients.

- The content i.e. what we say. The words you use are not the only thing other people pay attention to, but they are still important. Choose them carefully.
- The process i.e. how you say it. Be real with how you say things. Don't be fake or say something you don't mean. How we talk can make a big difference.
- The timing i.e. when you say it. Timing is everything, fam. Saying the wrong thing at the wrong time can totally mess up whatever you're trying to say. Pay attention to the situation and the people you are talking to. Permission. It's important to make sure that everyone involved is comfortable with what you are talking about. Asking for permission helps respect the person's boundaries. For instance, if you're talking to a friend and you keep interrupting him, he may feel like his thoughts or feelings aren't being valued. The right thing to say would be, "Is it OK if I share my own experience about this?" or "Would you be comfortable if I asked you a question about this?"

LISTENING IS COMMUNICATING

Have you ever been in a situation where you're talking to someone and they are on their phone, scrolling through reels non-stop? Or you are in a noisy coffee shop and the other person keeps on turning around to see who is entering every time the door opens. Isn't it a total vibe killer when it feels like the other person isn't even listening? You lose your flow, and the conversation seems forced.

The truth is active listening can be difficult. Our brains are programmed to pay attention to multiple things, even when we are trying to focus on the conversation. For instance, if you're talking to someone in a crowded place, your brain will try to block out the background, but it will still be hard to concentrate on what the other person is saying. To actively listen, we have to shut down all distractions and be fully present without letting our thoughts wander.

WHAT EXACTLY IS ACTIVE LISTENING?

Active listening involves being there fully in the moment when someone is talking to you, so you can actively hear the complete message that is being communicated. You need to avoid getting side-tracked, feeling bored, or thinking of ways to respond while the person is still speaking.

According to Susan Whitman, a board-certified life coach, and instructor at the University of Vermont, it "involves stepping into someone else's story, taking out your own judgments and opinions, and really listening to what is being said."

Active listening involves more than just hearing the words being said. You need to understand more than just the literal meaning of words. To do that, you must pay attention to various aspects, such as body language, facial expressions, and tone of voice.

The Three A's

Active listening has three elements, known as The Three A's. They are

- Attitude - non-judgmental and open-minded
- Attention - no distractions, looking around, glancing at phone, and so on
- Adaptability - flexible and willing to adjust if the conversation starts going in a different direction than you had planned

What are Active Listening Skills?

Whether you're chatting with your squad or trying to impress your teacher, these five listening techniques will help you level up your communication skills.

1. Pay Attention

When someone is speaking to you, stay focused. Look at the speaker's face, make eye contact, and put away all distractions, like your phone. Pay attention to their body language. Don't let your mind drift off to thoughts of what you're having for lunch, or how your crush is giving heart emoji vibes.

2. Show That You Are Listening

Use your body language and gestures to show that you are interested. Nod your head from time to time, make eye contact, raise your eyebrows, shrug your shoulders, and smile. Make sure you have an open and interested posture. Avoid crossing your arms and legs, face the person you're talking to, and tilt forward slightly. Verbally acknowledge by saying something like "yes", "uh-huh", "you're so right", or "no cap".

3. Reflect On What You Hear

Summarizing and repeating what the other person is saying will help you become a good listener. It allows you to show the speaker that you fully understand their point. Asking the speaker questions to clarify certain points is also helpful. You can say something along the lines of "Sounds like you are saying", "What I'm hearing is", or "Is this what you mean when you say".

4. Don't Interrupt

Isn't it frustrating when you're trying to make a point and someone cuts you off? Well, that's exactly what a good listener shouldn't be doing. Interrupting can prevent you from fully understanding what is being said. Listen to what the other person is saying without speaking up in the middle. Don't refute or come up with a counter-argument before the speaker is done. Try to keep an open mind and don't judge.

5. Respond Appropriately

It's important to respond thoughtfully and at the right time. Ask questions that allow the speaker to open up, such as "How did that make you feel?" or "What happened next?" It's ok to share your thoughts honestly but remember to be respectful.

Examples of Active Listening

Are you wondering how active listening spells out in real life? Here is an example:

Abby was upset about a fight she had with her bestie. She opens up to another friend, Nolan.
Abby: *I just had a big fight with Lisa last week. We haven't spoken to each other since and I'm so upset. I don't know what to do.*

Nolan: *That sounds really tough. Do you want to tell me about what happened?*
(asks an open-ended question)

Abby: *She's always been flaky but lately she's been canceling every plan we make. We planned to go watch the new Avatar movie together, I even got the tickets but she said she was not feeling that great and canceled last minute. But I know that was just an excuse. I saw Michael's Insta story and they were all having boba tea at the new coffee shop. I'm really hurt and I don't know if we should be friends anymore.*

Nolan: *I can see why you're upset. It's not cool for her to cancel plans and lie to you about it.*
(reflecting on what was heard)

Nolan: *How would you like to handle the situation?*
(asking an open-ended question)

Abby: *I'm not sure. Sometimes I want to tell her it's not ok, but I just don't want more drama in my life.*

Nolan: *Sounds complicated. I think it's good to be honest about your feelings. But don't do it as if you're attacking her. Maybe you could say something like, "Hey, can we sit and talk about something that happened the other day?"*
(offering an opinion without being judgmental)

Abby: *I think you're right. Thanks for listening- I just needed to vent.*

Here are some examples of what **NOT** to say:

- "That doesn't sound like a big deal, get over it"
- "I can't see why you're upset"
- "You're just overreacting"
- "I'm going through so much more but I don't complain"

It's important to ask open-ended questions, show empathy, and reflect on what the other person is saying by restating it in your own words. Here are some examples of active listening statements:

- "Sounds like you are mad about what happened the other day"
- "I just want to be sure I understand what you are saying"
- "I get how this could be hard for you"

ACTIVE LEARNING ACTIVITY

It's How They Say It

This is a small group Active Listening activity that you can do with some trusted friends. First, come up with a list of discussion topics and non-verbal cues. Divide the participants into small groups. Each group will get one discussion topic and a copy of the non-verbal cues list. Each person must secretly decide on the cue that best describes how they feel about their topic, and then do a 5-10 mime of their chosen cue. When they are acting, the others should each write down what they think the miming person feels about the topic. In the end, the miming person can reveal their cue and how they feel. Everyone can then compare notes to find out how accurate their interpretation was.

Here are some ideas for discussion topics.

- Fortnite is the best game ever
- TikTok is better than Instagram
- Pineapple on pizza is straight-up delicious
- Rap music is the best
- Parents should have their kids' passwords
- Homeschooling is better than traditional schooling
- There should be uniforms in every school

Here is a list of some non-verbal cues that the participants can choose from:

- Yawning
- Nodding
- Thumbs up
- Eye roll
- Facial expressions that show emotions such as being happy or sad
- Body language such as crossing your arms, leaning forward or backward in the chair

- Wide eyes
- Raised eyebrows

NOT TALKING IS ALSO COMMUNICATION

Communication is not just limited to what we say; it also includes the non-verbal cues that accompany our words. Standing too close to someone, touching them frequently, fidgeting with your hair or jewelry, and even biting nails give out the wrong non-verbal cues and can lead to misunderstanding, and make social interactions difficult.

WHAT IS NON-VERBAL COMMUNICATION?

Non-verbal communication includes our facial expressions, body movements, posture, eye contact, the tone and volume of the voice, hand gestures, and the distance between the two people who are talking. Non-verbal cues are like a special language of their own, and they give meaning to what we are saying. As you get better at communicating through non-verbal cues, it will be easier for you to interpret the other's person's cues and signals. Imagine being able to tell what the other person is thinking just by the way their hands move.

Types of Non-Verbal Communication

Some of the ways we use to communicate without words are:

- Body movements - Nodding or shaking the head, hand gestures such as a thumbs up /down, pointing to show direction, and patting someone on the back.
- Posture - how you stand or sit, how you keep your legs or arms.
- Eye contact - Prolonged eye contact may look too intense while avoiding it altogether can be seen as disinterest.
- Aspects of the voice - Pitch, volume, tone, and speed of speaking. It can be scary when the other person starts shouting.
- Distance from the other person - Don't get too close or too far. Respect personal space.
- Facial expressions - Smiling, raising your eyebrows, frowning, rolling your eyes, and grimacing.
- Changes in your body - Some of these may happen automatically and are impossible to control, for example, you may sweat or blink more when you are nervous.

Why Is It Important To Know Nonverbal Communication?

Sometimes, not saying anything can say a lot. How our bodies behave can give major signals about how we are feeling. Paying attention to non-verbal cues can improve our communication skills; it helps us interpret the other person's feelings and understand them better. Non-verbal cues and spoken words go hand in hand. We can't just look at one thing to get a better picture. We need to look at the full situation.

THE TEA ON BODY LANGUAGE

Body language is a part of non-verbal communication. It simply means the way we use our bodies to communicate. We use body language unconsciously, without thinking about it. Whenever you talk to someone, your body is constantly giving out signals, like the way you sit, the expressions you make, or the way your hands move. These signals affect the way other people interpret your words.

Sometimes, you may be saying one thing but your body language is saying something completely different. Have you ever experienced a time your friend told you she wasn't upset with you, but avoided eye contact and sat in a corner? You got the message she was mad at you, even though she said something else. When words and body language send different messages, people usually choose to believe the other person's body language, since it is a natural depiction of what they are feeling.

What Are Some Examples Of Body Language?

There are many ways to communicate through body language, such as

- Facial expressions like frowning, smiling, etc. The look on a person's face can reveal a lot about how they're feeling. Sometimes, our expressions are very brief and go away quickly. These are called "micro-expressions" and they usually happen when we are trying to hold back our emotions. Learning to spot micro-expressions can give you an edge in any interaction.
- The eyes can tell you a lot about a person's feelings. Paying attention to people's eyes is an important part of communication. Look out for how much they're blinking, whether they're looking directly at you or avoiding making eye contact, are their pupils getting smaller or bigger.
- The way someone moves their mouth is also a part of body language. For example, chewing on their bottom lip may mean someone is anxious. Pursed lips may be a sign of disapproval.
- Gestures are the most obvious form of body language. You can use your hands to give a variety of signals. For instance, giving an ok sign or thumbs

up means that you approve of the situation.
Rubbing your hands may show excitement, and
tapping your fingers is a sign of impatience.

- The way you place your arms or legs can give vibes
about how you feel. Crossing your arms or keeping
them close to your body will make you seem
unfriendly. If you cross your legs away from the
other person it shows you are uncomfortable in
their presence. The best bet is to keep your feet on
the floor.
- The way you sit, stand, or move your body shows a
lot about you. Sitting up straight shows confidence,
while hunching forward may make it seem like
you're bored.

Learning about body language can be a game-changer for
sure. Sending and reading the right signals helps you understand the other person's point, lets you come across the way
you want to, and allows you to bond. You know you've
unlocked squad goals when you and your bro can keep it
low-key and pick up on each other's vibe without saying a
single word.

MASTERING SMALL TALKS AND CONVERSATION

Small talk refers to light, informal conversation. It can be
thought of as a warm-up to the proper conversation. It's
commonly used when you're talking to someone you don't
know very well. Whether you're waiting in line at the

school cafeteria, attending a club meeting, or getting tickets to a movie, small talk is a valuable social skill.

It's completely normal to feel nervous about making small talk, especially with someone unfamiliar. But with a little practice, you can level up your small talk game. Here are some tips you can use to talk to anyone comfortably:

- Start with yourself. When you meet someone new, share something extra about yourself along with your name. You could try saying, "Hi! I'm Olivia. Here's a fun fact about me- I speak four languages"
- Talk about the weather. It's a cliché but it works every time.
- Stay woke in a positive way i.e. don't get preachy or try to police everyone but also keep yourself informed about what's going on in the world.
- Don't stress about the silence. Be comfortable with short pauses and start with a new topic.
- Take it to the next level. Build on a topic. If someone tells you they were at a concert recently, ask more questions. What songs were they playing, how many people were there, and how the experience was are some examples.
- Keep the don'ts in mind. Don't talk about controversial topics like politics and religion, don't ask personal questions and whatever you do, never give advice. Save deep convos for later.

ACTION STEPS

If you want to be on top of your communication skills, here are seven simple steps you can take.

1. Get Talking

It helps you make more friends and get through difficult stuff. The first step to making any progress is to get talking. Just keep doing it. Make it a habit. Start with people you don't know. Practice making small talk everywhere. Talk to the cashier, the Uber driver, the new guy in class, the cafeteria lady, the guy at the bus stop, the person next to you in the grocery line, the neighbor you sometimes run into, the jogger you encounter at the park. Many opportunities, you just have to take it on.

2. Kick Off A Conversation

So many ideas in this chapter. Pick one, pick any. It's the best way to understand people and build stronger relationships. Ask questions. Show some real interest. People like to talk about themselves, so use that. Look for something unique about them. Do they have a cool name? Are they wearing an interesting pair of shoes?

3. Listening Is Key

Don't just hear the words, actively listen and pay attention to what's being said. Ask open-ended questions and reflect on what's being said. People love talking about themselves especially if the other person is interested.

4. Feel The Mood

There is so much more than words happening when a conversation is taking place. Learn to decode nonverbal ways of communicating. Stop flexing and show some interest in other people. Be curious, pay attention, and don't make it all about yourself.

5. Give Compliments

It's a great way to break the ice. "Your fit is fire" will go a long way. Find things in common. If you notice someone wearing a Billie Eilish Tee shirt, talk about her latest album.

6. Observe

Read the other person's body language to fully get what they're saying. Do they look interested, bored, or want to respond to you? Be mindful of body language. Make sure your body is also saying what you want to say. Know when to end it. Wrap it up before it gets awkward. Try saying "It was cool talking to you. Catch you later."

7. Small Talk Leads To Bigger Things

Don't underestimate the power of talking about the weather. Small talk lets you start a conversation with anyone. It's a great way to get to know people better, and it lets you make new friends and have conversations. Who knows, that one simple question about someone's name could be the start of a lifelong friendship.

Communication matters, whether you're chilling with your friends, attending a party, or going shopping. It can help you feel less stressed and more connected to the people around you. When it comes to meaningful conversations, it's more than just the words you say. Body language can tell you a lot too. It's all about being there in the moment, paying attention, and actively listening. Don't be afraid to engage in small talk; it may seem intimidating but it can help you make more friends and build a bigger tribe.

4

IT'S TIME TO MAKE FRIENDS

The Only Way To Have A Friend Is To Be One

— RALPH WALDO EMERSON

va is a 17-year-old girl who is going to college in a few weeks. She spends her time reading young adult novels and scrolling through reels. FOMO hits her hard when she sees people throwing lit parties on Insta, but she is never invited. Her phone doesn't blow up with texts and memes. Shy and quiet, she's never had a big circle. But she made a few casual connections in school.

Before her freshman year, Ava's dad changed jobs and they moved to a different state. High school is tough, but being the new girl made it even harder. The first two years were awkward, and Ava was basically on her own She had no idea how to introduce herself or start a conversation. Even a simple "Hey!" became a struggle.

Things got so bad that she started spending her lunch breaks in the library, binge-reading the latest Colleen Hoover books. It helped her get over the embarrassment of sitting alone but earned her the "loner" tag.

In her Senior year, Ava's gym instructor convinced her to try out for the track and field team. Hanging out at the gym made her feel like she belonged. Ava finally felt she was a part of the family when her girls asked her to go shopping for Homecoming. But this did not last long, as her teammates started ghosting her after graduation.

Ava thought something was wrong with her. She felt like she was boring or people didn't like her because of her acne. Her low self-esteem made her resentful and she stopped leaving the house until she read an anonymous post on Instagram. Turns out, there are so many others who feel just like her. The anon poster post was sad no one called to check on them or had any friends to go to a concert with. They are the ones who never get a vibe check when they miss school for a few days, no one asks them about their day, and they have never danced to the latest Doja Cat song with their friends. Like Ava, most of these teens lack social skills. But there is hope - with a little effort, Ava can turn her L into a W But there's hope, with a little effort, Ava can turn her L into a W.

FRIENDSHIP SKILLS

Lyla and Kate have been friends since elementary school, but now they go to a different high school. Although they still hang out over weekends, both of them have started to feel that they don't have the same interests anymore. Lyla is more into activism and art, while Kate is interested in makeup and glam. They want to hang out with new kids at school. But they don't want to mess with their friendship.

Let's be real, making and maintaining friendships can be seriously tough. Social anxiety, awkward communication, and the pressure to fit into different crowds can leave you feeling stressed. If you want to build super strong bonds with your squad and handle drama like a boss, you need to level up your friendship skills.

What are Some Friendship Skills Everyone Needs?

Friendship skills are just social skills you need to make friends and to be a good friend. You need them to make friends, period. Having a squad that's always got your back can help you feel like you belong. It can shield you from haters and negative feelings. It teaches you values you will need your whole life such as trust, respect, kindness, and acceptance. By working on your friendship skills, you can deal with whatever tricky situations life throws your way.

No matter who you are, you can benefit from having a set of friendship skills under your belt. It can help you connect better with others and make you a good friend. When my older cousin was in high school, she had a friend called Jenna. Both the girls were always hanging out together, going shopping, or catching up over milkshakes at the diner. When my cousin got accepted into the music school of her choice,

Jenna straight-up ghosted her. When I asked my cousin about it, she seemed upset that Jenna didn't even say congrats and acted like she wasn't very happy about things. Both girls eventually talked it out, and Jenna realized that being happy for your friend is also a part of being a good friend.

If you don't want to make the same mistake Jenna did, and you are curious about friendship skills that can help you, check out these pointers:

Find The Right "Tribe"

Make sure you find people who accept and appreciate you, for who you are. Don't obsess over fitting into the cool crowd, even if they don't value you. Focus your energy on finding your real tribe. It doesn't have to be big; even if you find a few like-minded people, it's all good.

Smile

Bella was a 16-year-old who was insecure about her braces and hardly ever smiled. Everyone in class thought she had a RBF (Resting B**** Face). It became a major turn-off, and no one ever approached her. She felt left out until another girl in her class pointed it out to her. From then onwards, Bella started smiling more. She was surprised at how much more confident it made her and pretty soon she had become a part of a tight crew.

Teens like Bella don't realize that their "meh-face" gives other people negative vibes. Smiling is the ultimate hack.

It's not about smiling, to be honest, but rather pleasant. If people think you are in a bad mood, they avoid you.

Ask Questions

People love talking about themselves and asking questions is the easiest way to show them that you're interested in learning more about them. This way you may come up with something both of you can relate to.

Invite/Join

Be bold and make the first move. Invite someone to do something, or join a group activity. The next time you see the boys playing ball, ask if you can join them.

Share

Sharing things like books and pens is important, but you must learn to share the spotlight too. Let someone else soak up the attention. Don't monopolize the conversation and let others contribute to it. When you're talking about yourself, don't brag. Isn't it annoying talking to the other person when all they do is boast about their latest gadget or their new Air Jordans?

Celebrate, Don't Hate

Being happy for your friends and celebrating their wins is a way to show your friends that you care about what makes them happy. When they get a good score on the SAT, or they get into their dream college, don't get jealous. Instead cheer them on with a fist bump, "You go, girl!", or a fire emoji.

Coping Skills

Being able to handle tough emotions makes you a cooler person to be around. Nobody likes to hang out with the gym freak who throws a fit when they miss their fitness goals.

Solve Problems Like A Pro

When things don't go your way and drama happens, it's tempting to run to an adult. But it's cooler to handle your problems yourself. Talk about it, stand up for yourself, and find out ways to come up with a solution. Of course, rope in an adult if there is bullying, criminal activity, or something dangerous. Then you save your back.

Empathize

Empathy means putting ourselves in the other person's shoes and feeling what they are feeling. It's an important social skill, but it's so hard to learn that even some adults struggle with it. Being aware of your feelings, controlling them, and trying to imagine what the other person is feeling, are all skills that you must level up on if you want to become empathetic.

Striking Conversations

Being able to talk to people is an important social skill; it can be a lifesaver when you meet new people or when you are trying to impress your crush. To feel more confident when striking up a conversation, remember to keep it positive and start simple. Avoid talking about conversation killers such as politics and offensive jokes.

Have you ever had a cool convo that quickly turns into a snooze fest? Ending it politely without sounding rude is a crucial skill. The easiest way to do it is by being direct; you could excuse yourself by asking for directions to the restroom before moving on to meet other people.

FORD METHOD

The FORD method is an acronym for family, occupation, recreation, and dreams. It involves asking a set of universal questions about these topics. It is an easy way to start and keep a conversation going and helps you connect with other people.

How Does It Work?

The four areas that you can use to come up with questions are as follows.

Family

Since having a family is a universal experience, it's a good idea to have a list of family-related questions ready. They don't have to be elaborate, try asking simple questions such as:

- How is your mom/dad/grandma/aunty doing since the trip to the hospital/accident?
- Do you have siblings?
- What's your birth order?
- Do you play sports?

It's important to remember that family is a sensitive issue for some people. Don't ask personal questions that may make the other person uncomfortable, such as "Why don't your parents get along?" or 'How is your relationship with your dad?"

Occupation

Asking about someone's job is a sure thing to get the convo flowing. Admittedly, more of a grown-up thing, you can enquire about their summer jobs if they are doing one. If you are talking to a peer who's still in school, you can ask about academics. Some sample questions are:

- What's your favorite class in school and why?
- What are you planning to major in?
- Do you plan to take up a job over the summer break?

Don't cross boundaries or make the other person feel bad. Don't say things like "Why did you choose that school? It sucks!" or "Why didn't you get accepted into an Ivy League?"

Recreation

Asking people about what they do for fun or relaxation helps you learn about their interests. Build on the conversation and try to find a common interest to bond over. You can try asking

- What do you do to unwind?
- Have you watched any new shows/read any new books lately?
- How is your running coming along? Are you still training for the marathon?
- How was your hiking/trekking/beach/meeting family trip?

Avoid passing negative judgments about things others find fun. Don't make rude comments like, "You're into that! Isn't it boring?" or "What a weird way to kill time!"

Dreams

Asking someone about their dreams is a good way to go deep and have some real talk. You could try asking questions along the lines of

- Which place have you always wanted to travel to?
- What's your idea of a dream job?
- Where do you see yourself 10 years from now?

Talking about their dreams may not be for everyone. Asking about future plans can even make some teens uneasy, especially if they are in the process of figuring things out. It may take a few attempts to get the other person to open up. Avoid being pushy. Don't say things like, "That's unrealistic" or "You'll never be able to do that".

Shooting off one question after the other can make the conversation sound like a one-sided interview. Listen to what the other person is saying, and build on it by sharing your own experiences. To make your responses more interesting, explore new things, try different hobbies, and be passionate about something.

FRENEMIES & TOXIC FRIENDSHIPS

When my friend Lara was in middle school, she had a friend, Amy, who was always complimenting her to her face but mocking her behind her back. Some other friends tried to warn her, but she wouldn't believe them till she saw Amy's messages in a group chat. When Lara called her out, she denied it. Luckily, Lara had enough good friends around her and she was able to cut Amy out of her life.

Frenemies are the two-faced snakes in your circle who pretend to be your friends, just like Amy. They are mean, they put you down or manipulate you, and they leave you out. They are always talking bad about other people and it makes you wonder what they say about you when you are not around. They are never there for you but expect you to go above and beyond for them. Friendships turn "toxic" when you hang out with frenemies. Toxic friendships make you feel bad about yourself or others. They are all about drama with others.

If you have a toxic friend in your life, decide if you really want them around. If you do, talk to them about it. Shut them down clearly when they make bad comments about you; be witty but assertive. If you are done with all the drama, just walk away.

Cutting out toxic people feels liberating, but it can also be difficult especially if you don't have a big circle. Focus on building a new squad. Join an afterschool club or take up sports. Try to make friends from a variety of places, like school, the neighborhood, or the gym. Remember, life's too short to waste on fake friends; positive energy only.

WHEN SOMEONE DOESN'T WANT TO BE FRIENDS

Do you have this one friend that never hits you up on socials, always replies with a short "hmmmm" or an emoji when you text him, and is always canceling plans last minute? Chances are, he doesn't want to be friends anymore and this is his way of giving you a hint. Most people won't tell you that they are done being friends but you can always get an idea from their non-verbal cues.

When someone isn't interested in being friends anymore, the most obvious clue is that they don't want to spend time with you. They start ditching plans and make lame excuses. They won't engage with you on social media, will leave you on read, or reply with a quick shutdown. They don't show any interest in what's going on in your life, and don't update you on what's going on with them. They only connect with you when they need a favor.

If you find yourself dealing with this kind of a situation, try to clear up the misunderstanding. Tell them how you feel but don't use accusatory words, such as "You never have time for me". If that doesn't work, just let it be.

ACTION STEPS

1. Reflect And Evaluate

Ponder over your current friendship skills. Are there any skills that you struggle with, or any patterns that are holding you back from making friends? Do the same for your existing friendships. Are they healthy and fulfilling? Look for warning signs of toxic friendships. This needs to happen both ways. Analyze your own patterns as well as others.

2. Practice Talking

Work on your talking skills and take them to the next level. A smiling face is like a welcome sign. It can help you unlock any social situation by making you look approachable and friendly.

3. Ask

Learn how to use the FORD method to make the most of your social interactions. Pick one question from the categories shared and ask someone, today.

Host a gaming night and invite people you know who are into video games. Make plans to go to the music festival and ask your pals to join you.

4. Be Kind

Kindness is a good quality to have, and it goes a long way when you're trying to be friends. Not everyone knows how to be kind, but you can start practicing it in small easy steps. Do stuff for others, help a friend with homework, or offer to carry a neighbor's grocery. Offering compliments is also a form of kindness. So spread the love; it's the way to go.

5. Establish Boundaries

Set boundaries and cut off toxic friends. If it leaves you feeling uncomfortable, it is not meant for you. Surround yourself with people who make you want to be better versions of yourself, not reminders of what is wrong with you.

6. Practice Your Friendship Skills

Step out of your comfort zone. Build new connections with people who value you. Pay attention to how you display non-verbal cues. Ask open-ended questions, listen, and express interest. If talking to a room full of strangers makes you anxious, mentally prepare a list of things you can discuss beforehand and practice them. You can look up the small talk ideas given in the last chapter and build your conversation from that.

7. Be Patient

It takes time and effort to build good friendships. Don't lose hope when you don't see instant results.

Friends are everything, especially in those years when we identify ourselves with our peers. Not going to lie, some-times it's hard to figure out just how to make real friends that last. So expand your circle, build new connections, and use the FORD method to talk to anyone. These skills will not only help you make new friends but will also help you when you are working in a team.

HELLO, AND THANK YOU FOR PURCHASING MY BOOK!

Many readers are unaware of what a difference even one review makes.

I would greatly appreciate it if you could help other teens and parents of teens struggling with social skills find my book on Amazon by leaving a review.

It only takes 3 minutes, and I have made it easy for you to help!
Just click on the link below or scan the QR code with your phone.
I am very grateful for your support.

https://amzn.to/3QYxkqM

5

TOGETHER EVERYONE ACHIEVES MORE - T.E.A.M.

IMPORTANCE OF TEAMWORK

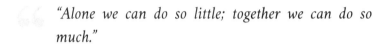 *"Alone we can do so little; together we can do so much."*

— HELEN KELLER

For 16-year-old Lucas, gaming was life. He was always up for a game of Fortnite or Overwatch. But he couldn't seem to avoid getting into drama. Every time he joined a game with his crew, there was always beef over strategy, loot, or straight-up trash talk. Lucas was legit hyped when he was invited to join a team for the High School Esports League. He was sure of his awesome gaming skills and felt super confident about winning.

But it was a total failure. Lucas was struggling to get along with his team which made them lose the first few games. He kept doing his own thing. His teammates were getting angry and tired of him, and some harsh words flew around. Lucas lost his cool and as he *responded to the digs, he made a really silly mistake. Things did not end well that day but fortunately, the team made it to the next round. They did not ask him to play that round though. Lucas walked out of the area huffing and puffing but once he found himself a quiet corner, and went over the events of the past hour, he felt like an amateur who was making rookie mistakes. Lucas and his supreme gaming skills were not really useful for his team. He had to do better the next time if he wanted to be a part of a team.*

Teamwork is crucial for success, whether it's on social media, online gaming, or on the field. Their stories serve as a reminder that no matter how talented you may be, to come out on top you need to have good teamwork and good collaboration skills. To understand what these skills are, read on.

TEAMWORK

Teamwork is the ability to work together to complete a common task. It's not just about dividing tasks, but also involves utilizing everyone's strengths to get the job done efficiently. Debates are a classic example of teamwork at play, where one member of the team might excel at research while the other is a persuasive speaker. Combining their strengths creates a winning argument. It's an essential skill that goes a long way. Learning how to work well in teams from an early age gives you a head start in preparing them for your future careers.

A good team must have certain characteristics. A team's success depends on how well the members bond together. Good communication helps tackle any issues that come up. Being able to share ideas openly and listen to each other makes it easy to work together. Another important thing for teams is commitment. When everyone is focused on achieving the same goals, they work hard to make it happen. Holding everyone accountable for their tasks helps them stay on track and get the job done.

Why You Need Teamwork

Have you ever noticed how kids who work well in teams get things done better than those who work alone? They can get the job done sooner and sometimes better. Working in a team helps develop many core social skills, such as empathy, cooperation, and tolerance. Teams are a great support system. Teamwork teaches core skills like problem-solving and leadership. It teaches you to express your ideas and opinions respectfully as well as respect other people's opinions.

Most importantly, teamwork boosts self-confidence by creating a supportive environment where you feel heard and valued. You feel like you are a part of a group that cares about you. When you feel like your opinions are taken seriously, you are more likely to speak up and engage in group discussions. What this also does is, it makes it hard for bullies to undermine your sense of worth. Teamwork also makes kids more empathetic toward kids who are being bullied. Kids who are team players are more likely to grow up into happy, successful adults.

If you don't think you are cut out to be a team player or don't have the skills, do not put yourself in a corner. As kids, we are born with the drive to have our basic needs for food and comfort met, and it's only through the lessons we learn in childhood that we begin to move away from that viewpoint. You will be forgiven for snatching a toy from your playmate, or bursting into tears if someone sits in your favorite chair when you were a toddler, over time, you will learn and get used to being part of a team.

FIVE TECHNIQUES FOR EFFECTIVE TEAMWORK

1. Individual Accountability And Responsibility:

Teams work well when everyone has clearly defined roles. It is important that group members agree on what has to be done and who is responsible for it. Everyone is responsible for their part of the pie. It is also important to have a clear understanding of each other's strengths. If you have a good artist on the team, insisting they pitch in and do one-quarter of the research is not equality. Asking them to design the layout, cover page or illustrations of your report might be more useful. The workload should be divided in a way that no one is overburdened and everyone can pitch in.

2. Constructive Feedback:

Team members give and receive feedback. The idea is to put your opinion forward in a constructive and productive manner. You can do this by listening, asking questions for clarity when appropriate, and being receptive to new ideas and changes. Accepting feedback is as important as giving it. Use respectful words when communicating your thoughts instead of shooting down ideas before they are completed. Phrases like, "Can we talk about this idea more?" "I am not sure if this will capture all the points" might be more useful than "This is so lame".

3. Problem-Solving:

Problems will occur and conflict will likely happen but teams that work efficiently understand that they need to resolve it all amicably. A heated argument or disagreement within will not get the results. If you foresee a problem or encounter it, brainstorm and present your solution. Be graceful when someone else gives a better suggestion.

4. Management And Organization:

a team is as good as its weakest link. This means everyone works together to add value. All teams have a leader (even if it is not said out loud). Different members have different functions. One person leads the discussion, one ensures deadlines are met, and the other one can be in charge of putting it all coherently. Knowledge of your role is essential. Good teams are also willing to rotate roles to maximize their own and others' group learning experience. All teams almost always have that one person who talks a lot and one person who makes sure everyone stays focussed!

5. Healthy Group Dynamics:

For a team to function well, there needs to be a sense of cohesion among the members and every team member is responsible for upholding the dynamics. This can come via the following:

- **Openness:** you don't need to be best friends with your teammates but you must be open to getting to know one another, especially those with diverse experiences and interests. This is very very relevant in long terms group activities and especially sports. It helps if you are receptive to fresh perspectives, different points of view, and the variety of people in the group. Understanding them and their situation can help you bond better.
- **Trust:** All teams should provide a sense of camaraderie and trust. Group mconstructively and productively one another to express their own thoughts and emotions without getting judged or mocked. They should not worry about being ostracised by their teammates if they miss a goal or make a wrong pass.

- **Support:** Good team members show support for one another as they complete their tasks. They serve as an example of team loyalty by supporting the group as a whole and assisting members who are having problems. They see one another as partners rather than as rivals.
- **Respect:** Group members communicate their opinions in a way that respects others, focusing on "What can we do better next time?" rather than "Who is to blame?"

WHAT MAKES A SUCCESSFUL TEAM

Teammates must be able to communicate well on an intellectual and emotional level to work well in small groups. This means:

- can explain their own ideas
- express their emotions in a direct but non-aggressive manner
- pay close attention to others on the team
- ask clarifying questions to ensure everyone is on the same page
- initiate conversations if they sense tensions brewing

Successful teamwork requires constant open communication in which participants express their thoughts, ideas, and feelings. Unspoken presumptions and problems can seriously hinder effective group functioning. Open dialogue will foster a positive environment and allow for success.

COLLABORATION SKILLS

Being able to work well in a team is a super important skill that you can use in school, college, and your work life. Collaboration skills are equally important.

Teamwork typically refers to a larger group of people working together on an ongoing basis with roles and tasks that are clearly defined. Collaboration typically involves a smaller group working closely together on a specific project. It involves cooperating, and sharing ideas, and skills to finish a task. It's more than just working on a project with others. People who have good collaboration skills know how to bond with their team, how to fix problems and create a winning combination. The term to remember here is synergy i.e. a combined effect greater than the sum of the separate effects.

Collaboration is like making a TikTok dance with your crew. Everyone has their style and they bring their flavor to the video, but when all of you work together, it creates magical content. It's all about sharing ideas, practicing, and gelling together. Don't be the one who throws off the whole routine by doing your own thing. Stick to the script and don't start doing your own thing to outshine the others just because you know the steps better.

Why Do You Need Collaboration Skills?

Collaboration skills are like a secret cheat code for unlocking epic achievements together as a squad. Here are the reasons why being a good team player is crucial for success.

- Working with your squad helps you discover and use each other's strengths to come up with great results while learning interesting things along the way. Imagine being on a group project with a techie and a research wizard. The final presentation will be straight-up awesome!
- You learn to see things from different points of view by working together. This helps you respect the other person's opinion even if it's different from yours and makes the world a more peaceful place.
- Working with your team lets you build soft skills that your teachers and future bosses are into. Learning to work with a crew will teach you to do better in your school and career goals.

NEGOTIATION SKILLS

Let's be real. How many times have you had to convince your parents to relax your curfew? Or to let you get your eyebrow pierced or your hair dyed neon pink? Have you ever had to negotiate where to go for dinner when one of your friends wants tacos and the other wants Thai? Have you ever decided on fair rules for family game night? Learning to negotiate without getting riled up is key to getting your way while making sure everyone is happy.

What is Negotiation?

Negotiating is a major life skill. It's a skill that goes beyond picking which movie to watch, or which mall to go to. It involves being able to listen to other people, understand their perspectives, and find a way to make things work for everyone. It isn't just about winning while leaving the other person hanging. Successful negotiation involves finding common ground and looking for a win-win solution for everyone involved.

When my teenage cousin wanted to go to a concert with her friends, her parents were very hesitant about it. It was in a different city an hour away and felt that at 14, she was too young to stay in a hotel overnight. So she sat down and negotiated like a pro. Her parents told her about their reservations over safety and transportation. After some give and take, they struck a deal. Her dad offered to let her stay at the concert for as long as she wanted if she agreed to call him when it was over and he would pick her up at night. The other terms included regular check-ins, keeping her location switched on, and calling if she felt uncomfortable for even a moment. In the end, it was totally worth it.

Negotiation skills are something you start practicing at a young age, even before you realize it. For instance, when you're playing with your friends and you need to decide who gets to be "it", or when you need to share a toy with a sibling, your negotiation skills are at work. I'm sure most of you have had to negotiate with your parents about getting a cookie before dinner or chicken nuggets for lunch. These small situations help build the foundation for more complex negotiations in the future, such as negotiating with bosses about work hours and pay rates.

Why Should You Learn to Negotiate?

Negotiation is a power move that helps you figure out who you are, what you want and believe in, and where you fit in. Learning how to negotiate is like learning any other new skill; it takes time and effort to become a boss at it. When you argue with your parents, negotiate a deadline with your teachers, or get into it with your friends over which show to watch, it's a chance to practice your negotiation skills in a healthy way.

You are more likely to show your buddies that you care about their feelings and listen if you are good at negotiating. This can make you build better connections with your friends. Being a boss negotiator helps you take on all the struggles of being a teen, whether it's dealing with peer pressure, relationships, or school stress.

Five Steps To Ace Negotiations

If you want to ace the negotiation game, here are some tips:

1. Get Involved

The best way to learn negotiation is by getting involved in decision-making at home. Ask your parents to let you have a say in negotiable stuff like chores, activities, and the weekly menu. Don't forget that some things are non-negotiable like going to school, curfew rules, and allowances. So speak up and flex those negotiation muscles. You will feel more in control when your voice is heard. Do the same with friends. Not everything has to be a negotiation but once in a while suggest a place to eat or a movie to watch. If you feel strongly about something, say the words.

2. Don't Force Your Take On Others

Imposing your opinion on others will make them defensive and quick to lash out. Let the other person talk and share their side of things. Tell them to hit you up with questions and respond with patience and empathy. If three out of five friends want to watch a particular movie, go with the mood of the majority.

3. Take It Easy

Negotiating can sometimes feel like you're in a battle. But going in with all guns blazing will only make it worse. Avoid getting upset or starting a fight. Curb your emotions and keep your cool. If you want your parents to take your opinion seriously about going to a party, instead of screaming, "I'm going whether you like it or not", try saying "I really want to go, but I understand where you're coming from. Can we talk about it?

Practicing what experts call, "Negotiation Jujitsu" is a good way to turn a negative into a positive by keeping your calm. Instead of getting sucked into an argument, don't react and figure out what everyone else wants.

4. Be An Active Listener

When the other person is talking, don't interrupt. Give everyone a chance to speak. This way, everyone feels heard and it's easier to resolve issues. To make sure you're on the same page as everyone else, try repeating what they say. It is not about winning the argument or having your suggested place picked. The idea is to do something that works for everyone, not just you.

5. Vibing vs Fighting

Remember, negotiating isn't about coming on top or taking a loss. It's about finding common ground where everyone is cool with the outcome. Be willing to give a little to get what you want. If your friend wants to watch movie A and eat at place B, a probable suggestion is to watch the movie of his choice and eat at the place of your choice. This way, both get what they want. Additionally, respect the decision. Don't crib through the duration of the movie because unpleasantness, like the flu, is contagious. You are out to have a good time, not be a downer.

ACTION STEPS

Are you ready to take action and achieve those goals? Dive into these action steps.

1. Take Up A Team Sport

This could be football or basketball. Have fun on the field while leveling up your communications skills and leadership game.

2. Do Group Projects

Make a presentation or come up with a video. Use apps like Google Docs to stay on top of your group tasks. Find something fun to work on, like making a YouTube video or planning a party or a camping trip.

3. Join A Club

Connect with people who have the same interests as you. Build your skills while having a blast in drama or music club. Check out online opportunities to do the same. Join an online forum or participate in social media activities that require you to work with someone else.

4. Volunteer

Show some love for your community while learning team skills. It's therapeutic because helping others really builds character. It also allows you to be a part of something that is bigger than you.

5. Team Building Activities

Take part in team-building activities with your team like an escape room or a scavenger hunt where everyone has to work together as a team.

6. Start At Home

Offer to help out with chores, like cooking with the family where everyone has their own set of responsibilities. Family game nights are a great way to hone these skills.

7. Don't Be A Hater

Respect everyone's opinions and don't force your views on them. Look back on your teamwork skills, and figure out what you need to work on.

As the quote at the start of this chapter clearly said, together we can do so much. When you team up, you can do the impossible and win the game. It's like magic! So practice your skills. Lucas would have been fine on his own too but the opportunities he would have gotten and the games he would have played with a team wouldn't come from playing solo.

Lucas did realize where he was lacking: being good at the game wasn't enough; he needed to be a good team player. Lucas did not wait for the next tournament to show his skills. He made an active effort to get along with the other member. He started talking to his teammates and paid attention to their ideas and strategies. He respected their opinions during the matches they had and it was not long before he got picked for the next tournament. Lucas finally found his groove in the gaming world. His team did not win the finals, but he found himself a team that had many many wonderful moments together!

6

ALL IS BIG UNTIL IT IS SOLVED TO BECOME SMALL

NO PROBLEMS, JUST SOLUTIONS

M ia, an Instafamous 16-year-old, was excited to work on her first-ever Insta collaboration with another equally stellar influencer. She thought it was going to be fantastic but it turned out to be a major let down. Both the girls had different auras and aesthetics. It was like trying to put up two filters on the same picture. They tried to come up with content but it turned out to be a mess. The collaboration fell through, and Mia was left feeling upset.

Mia was heartbroken for days. She thought her channel was going to disappear soon and all her followers would dump her. She checked her texts, DMs, and her locker incessantly for hate mail. She even checked the mailbox though no one sends anything by snail mail anymore. She cooked up the worst of scenarios and would fly to her room as soon as she got back from school. In school, she would keep her head down and avoid her peers because *as far as she was concerned, the entire world was laughing at her behind her back. Life was over and her page was going to die soon.*

Mia was in a predicament, like many of us. It's more common than most of us would like to think. We mistake problems as failures and demote ourselves. We envision something to be bombastic and instead it just bombs. Happens with our projects, actions, even our jokes and fashion sense. We are not perfect and holding us to those high standards is overrated.

Should she let this one setback ruin all the hard work she had put in through the months? Should she wallow in tears and hide for the rest of her life or try to figure out what went wrong so it doesn't happen again?

As soon as you change the way you view things, there is potential to find solutions. Projects fail, not people. Problems, on the other hand, are opportunities to change the situation. They are little obstacles that you encounter on the way to doing awesome things. Change the way you view it and you might actually change the outcome.

PROBLEM-SOLVING SKILLS

In the years between childhood and adolescence, you are going to learn a lot of skills you will need as an adult. You should start working on independent problem-solving now, because the sooner you master it the better. Even when you make mistakes, you are still learning, because in a way you know what not to do in the future.

Everybody should be able to solve problems, and your approach will determine whether or not you are successful. The problem could be little or significant, like finding your way home from a neighbor's house, asking the sales rep if you can try a different size, or leaving an uncomfortable situation at a party.

Problems are a normal part of life and the thing about them is that it greatly affects and influences how you feel. Some problems may make you frustrated, angry, resentful, or plain sad. They might also make you feel so terrible that you feel like quitting. You may prefer avoiding the issue altogether instead of spending time solving it

But what if I told you that problems are what you make of them? You can think of them as problems that are beyond your control. You can also think of them as obstacles that you can overcome, like a puzzle that must be solved. You have a choice and this chapter is all about exercising the power of choice that lies within.

How you feel about them is down to your willingness and capacity to solve them. The answers are rather evident in some situations because you already know what to do and how to solve the issue. In other circumstances, the solutions are not obvious, and you must weigh a wide range of alternatives before selecting the most appropriate one.

The ability to solve problems is crucial for surviving the challenging teenage years and will be useful throughout your life. Every day, whether at school, work, or in a social setting, we are all faced with solving challenges. You will gain the ability to resolve disagreements, be independent, difficult tasks, and make decisions on your own by developing problem-solving abilities.

The amusing bit is we have the skills, we just don't know how to use them in some places. If you are facing a bunch of problems in life (absolutely normal, and in fact, life would be a boring flat line if it weren't for problems), let me tell you about the two types of skills you need to solve problems.

CRITICAL THINKING

Critical thinking, also referred to as logical reasoning, is the ability to analyze and assess an issue by breaking it down into smaller parts. If the term terrifies you, just keep in mind that you already know it. Don't believe me? Well, mathematical skills like sorting, categorizing, and contrasting similarities and differences are part of critical thinking.

Have you ever jumped from the kitchen counter? Around the age of 4 or 5, you had some sense of what height to jump from if you did not want to get hurt. That's how far back making sound decisions that are reasoned and well-thought-out go.

Need some more insight? When you were younger and your mom poured the juice into two glasses, for you and your sibling, you compared the two to figure out which one held more. That was you using your critical thinking skills.

That was you as a child. You use this rather fancy-sounding skill in your older years as well. You stopped believing in Santa and knew it was Mom and Dad and not the tooth fairy who left goodies under your pillow. Then you grew more and stopped believing every justification and conclusion you heard from your parents.

You argue/debate/readjust the rules they have set. You negotiate terms to get your own cell phone. You bargain for additional screen time for the weekend. You insist you get your own social media account/own room/increase in allowance or delay in curfew for special nights out by using concrete and well-balanced explanations to support your agenda. You, yes you, already are a critical thinker. You just need to expand your sphere.

CREATIVE THINKING

Creative problem-solving is the first step. It is the ability to think up original ideas, use materials in creative ways, and view situations from a different angle. Creative thinking requires the willingness to take risks, try new things, and even make errors. In fact, so often, it is our errors that compel us to look at things from a different angle. Creative thinking includes "fluent" thinking, which is the ability to generate or brainstorm ideas. It is the ability to ask and answer open-ended questions that allow you to think about things in more than one way. It is a departure from the "yes and no type of questions".

If creative thinking reminds you of all the times the teacher asked you to be creative in school, and you shudder at the thought, remember this is also a skill set you have even if you did not get a good grade on those essays.

When you were younger and used the spoon or the hairbrush as a microphone and sang like you were participating in American Idol, you had figured out a novel way to use a mundane item. When you answered questions like all the things that are red (fire truck, fire, mom's shirt, your favorite glass) you imagined all the things that could be red and did not limit it to ladybugs; When you wore your dad's shirt around your neck and pretended it was a superhero cape, you pushed the boundaries of your imagination; when you donned mom's heels so you could reach the top counter, you thought of different ways to solve the old problem.

It doesn't stop there. Have you ever discussed your curfew time with your parents so you can go to the lit concert with your friends? You think you are old enough to go but of course, you need permission, and you question the decisions. You come up with creative solutions - you talk about how you will update them regularly, go with friends the parents know, or leave enough information so they can track you down. Negotiation skills, discussed earlier, are an example of creative thinking - you negotiate the terms You are wearing the critical thinking hat - you don't accept the rules made by them at face value, understand what their reservations are and suggest solutions that will ease their worries. At the concert, you accept drinks from your friends only and not from strangers you have just met (critical thinking).

This is problem-solving - one facet is about making decisions that are well-thought-out and grounded in logic and the other facet is creative flexibility where you consider various options to do the same thing. When you are in a pickle, there are options available, it's a matter of accessing them.

FIVE STEPS OF PROBLEM-SOLVING

The following steps will help you solve most of the problems with ease:

1. Identify The Issue

The first step is to identify the problem. Ask yourself about the current situation and what you would like it to be. Simply saying the words out loud can help too: "I need to improve my math grade," "I don't have anyone to sit with at lunchtime," or "I am not sure if I should speak to the teacher about my group project".

2. Think Of At Least Five Possible Solutions

Consider all the potential solutions to the issue. Insist on the fact that not all solutions have to be intelligent (at least not at this point) but they have to be realistic. If you are running late for school every day, you cannot consider flying to school as a viable option. You can however consider these options: waking up early; preparing everything the night before; setting the clock forward by a few minutes or having an extra alarm for leaving the house. Going to bed dressed up may not be viable but you can include it for some laughs! The intention is to understand that you can come up with a range of workable solutions with a little creativity.

3. Identify The Pros And Cons Of Each Solution

Identify potential positive and negative consequences for each potential solution. Imagine what may happen if you use that specific solution. Weed out options where the disadvantages exceed the advantages or the ones that don't seem to be workable this will help you select the best course of action.

4. Pick A Solution

Implement the idea that can resolve the crisis. Give it your best and see how it works.

5. Test It Out

Check out a solution and see how it works. They can always try the next option if the first one doesn't work out.

Finally, assess the result. Some problems take longer to be solved. Likewise, sometimes you can't solve a problem in a single go. Don't be disappointed and give up, rather attempt another option from the list you created in step two. Explore all options and have a backup plan. Ask yourself what has or hasn't worked well and what can be done differently to make the solution work more smoothly.

RESOLVING CONFLICT

Eli, the footballer from the previous chapter struggled with his on-field repertoire with teammates but it often carried off-field too. He would get personally offended if someone commented on his game or the pass he missed. He would snap back on some days and spiral. It was affecting his performance and the overall morale of the team. Moreover, getting enraged with the coach or the players of the opponent team was beginning to earn him a bad reputation. This constant state of conflict or anger is not good for anyone.

No one enjoys conflict but arguments, disagreements, and even bitter incidents are an inevitable fact of life. They can range from minor conflicts, like when you were a kid and engaged in a tussle with a friend or sibling (He grabbed my toy car) to major ones (using inappropriate language on the field or being told, "I don't want to be your friend anymore").

As you grow up and interact with people without your parents being around, chances are you will have to solve them on your own. You might be someone who is more confrontational than others or someone who finds themselves in these kinds of circumstances more frequently. The annoying thing about conflicts is that they are more likely to occur for people who like taking immediate action, although passive behavior can also harm relationships and create resentment in future interpersonal relationships. The not-so-annoying this about conflict, however, is how we react to it is our choice. Conflict need not feel disastrous, even though it may be unpleasant.

It is important to learn conflict resolution skills to settle disputes when they arise. Moreover, they also come in handy to stop disputes before they get out of hand. You need to learn not only how to resolve disagreements, but also how to express yourself, respectfully make your point, set limits, and be assertive while avoiding conflicts.

Let's say a classmate constantly picks on you or makes mean comments about your clothes or your physical attributes. You need to define the boundaries and communicate that it is not acceptable. Creating boundaries in this scenario might lead to more conflict, but it might be necessary to ensure that you are standing up for yourself. If someone chooses to escalate a dispute, it is not really your responsibility but there are a few things you can do to maintain your end of the stick. Remember that when things go awry, both of you will be called to the principal's office!

FIVE STEPS OF CONFLICT RESOLUTION

These strategies can assist in limiting confrontations:

1. Stop

Take a step back. Remove yourself from the place of conflict, albeit momentarily to collect your thoughts. Attacking a problem head-on, in the heat of the moment isn't always a good idea. No problem was ever resolved when tempers were flaring.

If you cannot physically leave the room, breathe in and out for a few seconds. Mindful breathing (discussed later in this chapter) is a helpful technique to detach yourself from the situation and calm down.

2. Say

Mention the problem out loud. Use words to describe what the conflict is about. Make sure you both have a clear understanding of what is causing the disagreement and clarify what each of you wants or doesn't want.

3. Think

Consider the issue at hand. Was it right? Was it unfair for one party? What would be a just answer that satisfies the needs of both parties?

4. Choose

Suggest and pick an option that both parties can agree on.

5. Respect

Even if you disagree, respect other people's opinions.

These are some guidelines but of course, there will be situations where the other party is not looking for a resolution, just some conflict. If that's the case., and you feel like you are being unnecessarily targeted, or bullied, it is best to contact a trusted adult. This could be an empathetic teacher in school, your parents, or even the coach of your sports team. There is always someone out there to help, you just need to ask. If you are wondering when it's bullying, here are some guidelines to help you gauge the scenario:

SIGNS IT'S BULLYING

While it's not always simple to spot the warning signs of bullying, take comfort in the knowledge that you can alleviate the situation if you have conflict resolution skills.

Bullies can be found in schools, playgrounds, social interactions, and even at home. They are on the internet as well where cyberbullies can use the anonymity of the forum to call you names or spread stories about you. If you are repeatedly experiencing any of the following, it is best to speak to an adult:

- Name-calling
- Physical altercation - pushing, nudging, tugging, and even throwing your belongings away can be classified as a physical alternation if done repeatedly
- Interrupting/Refusing to listen
- Insulting your intelligence (mocking, mimicking)

EFFECTIVE COMMUNICATION

You need to learn to express your emotions in clear ways without yelling or accusing if the plan is to resolve the problem. It is challenging to exercise restraint when you are in the middle of a fight so try to practice some of these tips when things are calm and eventually, you will get the hang of it.

- Use "I" statements. Talk about how the action makes you feel. Starting sentences with "you" can come across as aggressive and they automatically put the other person on the defensive. Say something like "I was embarrassed when you called me a geek in front of everyone" instead of "You called me a geek to embarrass me". "I did not like it when you told the teacher I don't like presentations" will be more helpful than, "You told on me for laughs".

- Write down what you plan to say. This may seem frivolous but if something has been bothering you for a while and you want to put an end to it, just write down a few lines of what you plan to say in a notebook. Let's say you have a classmate who fist bumps real hard or puts their hand around your shoulder every time you guys have a chat. If you don't like it, consider telling them the issue. The idea is to tell them you don't like that one particular action. This will allow you to get your thoughts through successfully.

- Role-playing with an adult. Tell them the context and what you plan to say. This solves two problems - you have a trusted adult who knows the situation and can guide you about what you are saying. They might even give additional insight. What if you communicate the issue but do so with hands folded or in a condescending tone? As we already know, non-verbal cues can play a role in how your message is received and a third party can provide valuable feedback.

ACTIVITIES TO DO

You can learn how to handle conflict in a regulated way through family and peer interactions. The following are a few exercises that you can undertake during regular social interactions to practice conflict resolution and emotional resilience:

1. The Emotion Thermometer

A quick Google search will help you understand this concept. The emotion thermometer is simply a thermometer with numbers but instead of telling you if you have a fever or not, it helps you gauge your emotions. Try to see where you stand (red hot angry, orangish nervous, nervous, calm, or happy). Based on the number/color, decide whether you need to calm down before proceeding. With some practice, you will be able to simply visualize the stoplight or thermometer in your mind to assess your emotional state. This awareness will help you understand yourself better.

2. Problem-Solving Baseball

If you have a problem, do a bit of mental baseball. The first base is identifying the problem so you ask yourself, "What is the problem". The second base is, "What are some potential options?" Third base identifies the best options. And home base is, "Am I safe or out?" "Did I pick the right option?"

The object is to understand what is going to get you closest to your goal.

3. Meditation

This is a great way to train your mind to be more responsive and less reactive. There is science behind it too. The amygdala is a part of the brain that deals with stressful situations and gets activated when we are nervous (it produces stress hormones). The frontal lobe is the part where rational decision-making happens. Meditation helps us train our brain to use the frontal lobe i.e. the calm dude instead of the amygdala i.e. the stressed-out dude. This training, however, requires a bit of meditation. There are many ways to meditate and a simple exercise is outlined below to get you started:

a. Find a quiet, comfortable spot to sit or lie down. You can sit cross-legged, on a chair, or lie on your back with a tiny pillow under your head The idea is to get into a comfortable position.
b. Close your eyes or softly gaze at your lap or straight ahead and pay attention to your breathing
c. Inhale slowly and deeply through your nose. Keep your shoulders relaxed.
d. Exhale slowly through your mouth. As you blow air out, purse your lips slightly but keep your jaw relaxed. Pay attention to each breath as it comes and goes.

e. You will have a lot of thoughts while you do this. It is okay. Acknowledge your thoughts and then gently bring your attention back to your breath. Some people count their breaths to stay focused. Think of it like riding a bicycle - you look at things you cross without really stopping.
f. Pay attention to your chest and abdomen, and how they contract and expand. Notice how the breath feels on the nostrils, breathing in and out.

Your mind is always thinking but when you slow down your breathing, you slow down your thinking which ultimately helps you feel calm. Start small with four to five minutes of meditation, with the goal of advancing to 15 minutes, once a day, four to five times a week. Some experts say it takes three weeks to make the transition and there is only one way of verifying that claim!

ACTION STEPS

1. Ask The Right Questions

We've all encountered situations where we want to learn more, yet all we receive is a cursory one-word response. Usually, the answer is "yes" or "no". The trick is to ask open-ended questions. "Do your like football?" versus "What sports do you like?" will fetch you a better answer. " Do you really think that's a good idea in this situation?" versus

"How would that work in this situation?" A reply to an open-ended question requires more thought. And that leads to real communication. Practice asking these questions when you get the time

2. What Would You Do If

This is actually a card game where you are presented with several commonplace everyday situations. You don't need to buy it though to practice it. The idea is to get thinking of different scenarios and strategize how you can make good choices when you encounter one. Think of the scenarios that keep you worried or the kind of problems you think might fact and then devise a way to get out of it. You can also search the internet for ideas. The trick is to have a general problem and not very specific. Instead of thinking of comebacks if someone calls you fat, plan the response when you are called a rude name. What would you say if you are late for class? How would you react if you trip? Should you laugh it off or stay like a statue till someone offers to help? Or gather your belongings and rush out? Just be careful and don't be fixated on problems. Think of good things too!

3. Listen

The ability to listen is crucial to problem-solving abilities. Listen without disputing or arguing. Listen without formulating a response in your head. Listen without judging or reading too much into the conversation. Express yourself using statements like "I need, I want, and I feel".

4. Determine If You Can Trust Them

Sometimes people will lie, which can make things more difficult, but point number 3 becomes much simpler if you can trust the person on the other side.

Unless they're genuinely lying, trusting the other party makes it easier to understand and accept what is being said but what do you do if they are not trustworthy and lying about things? You actually need to spot contradictions in what they are saying or being dishonest because it changes the dynamic of the conflict resolution. In fact, it might be more productive to take a step back to readjust to the new narrative. For conflicts to be resolved, you need to be operating with the same set of facts.

5. Know Your Conflict Resolution Style

Spend some time reflecting on the disputes in your life thus far and try to identify your preferred method of handling them. Even if you're a little heated and upset, do you prefer to deal with it right away? Do you believe that's the best course of action, and how well did it perform for you in the past?

6. Don't Hit Below The Belt

This one needs to be read twice. The teen/preteen years are not easy and you will encounter people with a mean streak. What if you are in an argument and the person starts making personal attacks or says things trying to egg you on or frustrate you? How will you respond? Are you going to respond in the same tone? Will you start yelling back? Using similar mean names? Although it may feel great to join in on the mudslinging, it is incredibly counterproductive to the situation. Keep the tone steady, avoid below-the-belt comments, and resist the urge to lash out. It may feel like you are losing the battle but you will come out of it in a better position.

7. Learn The Different Variations Of Mindful Breathing

There are different ways to breathe and each has its own particular benefit. Familiarize yourself with the different ways. Practice the breaths the next time you take a shower or get ready for bed. One technique, known as box breathing is mentioned here:

- Count to 4 as you inhale
- Hold the air in your lungs for a count of 4
- Exhale to a count of 4
- Hold your lungs empty to a count of 4
- Repeat this pattern at least 3 to 5 times

There is always a solution, you just need to look for it. Let's talk about Mia again. Mia decided to make a choice. Instead of seeing it as the end of her page, she took a brief break and returned to the situation. She asked questions and some of them were tough: Had she failed or had that one content failed? Was it going to matter in a few days? She realized that being an influencer wasn't just about followers and posting content, she needed to post stuff that interested her followers.

Collaborating with a swanky influencer may look good on paper but the content had to appeal to her fan base, the people who had been liking and subscribing to her channel. They liked pop and the concert they had covered was more rock in terms of genre. The influencer she collaborated with had a different target audience and it did not match her audience's taste. This also meant understanding that it wasn't the other party's fault. She had unfairly blamed her for this mess. She worked on her communication skills, understood the scenario and soon enough had devised a plan to move forward and roll out content that really mattered. Of course all this required action, along with gaining a clear understanding of her own emotions. How you really do that is discussed in detail in the upcoming chapter!

7

DODGING THE EMOTIONAL TRAP

MANAGING EMOTIONS AND FEELINGS

S arah, 13, wakes up on Monday morning, well-rested and looking forward to the day ahead. She enjoys school, and the excitement of presenting that history project - the one she had been working on for weeks - pumps her up. She can't wait to see what her teacher thinks of her work.

As she gets ready, the butterflies of excitement in her stomach start fluttering around in big, nervous tremors. What if her research wasn't good enough? What if she froze in front of the entire class? Was there something on her teeth? Definitely not having breakfast now!

As she sits through her history class watching everyone present in turns, the nerves kick into overdrive. The boy she has had a crush on is sitting right in front and now she is rethinking everything, from the topic she chose to the way she decided to do her hair. She starts fidgeting and can almost see her classmates sitting around to see what she is up to. Oh for this day to be over!

But as soon as she begins, everything fades away and she kicks into confident-Sarah mode. She's well-prepared, the presentation is well-made and researched thoroughly, and everyone seems genuinely interested in what she has to say. As she nears the end, an overwhelming sense of relief washes over her and she can't help feeling proud of herself. What a high!

Sadly, that feeling doesn't stick around for long either. There is a surprise quiz during math that she is not prepared for. This left her feeling utterly miserable to the point that she took offense at a very casual joke her friend made. Sarah made a quick retort and left the table.

As she walked home, Sarah recounted every detail of her conversation with the friend and what she should have said instead of what she said. She had forgotten about the presentation completely and was fixated on the not-so-pleasant moments of the day.

By the time she got home, the roller coaster of emotions had taken the wind out of Sarah. She was angry, annoyed, and flustered, and the last thing she needed was to recount the day's events to her very interested mom. She mumbled an incoherent reply to her questions, stomped upstairs to her room, and slammed the door shut. All she wanted to do was scroll through TikTok and watch funny videos to take her mind off everything. And maybe post a nice selfie on Instagram – her hair still looked good.

Midway through all this, Mom showed up to call her down for dinner and happened to see the state of the room. She commented on the clutter that just pushed Sarah off the edge. Doesn't her mom realize how tough her day had been? Why can't she be nicer and more understanding? Sarah yelled at her mom to leave her alone and rushed to the door to close it. Even though she was the one who yelled, tears come down, thick and fast, and she lay on her bed face down, weeping into her pillow, until her throat was dry and her face was swollen.

Sarah experienced just about every emotion through the course of the day and as normal as that is, it is the intensity of her emotions that wasn't right. Or appropriate. Emotions are a normal part of everyday life and all of us experience them in different ways. Getting something we have wanted for a while makes us happy, getting caught in traffic annoys us, and doing poorly on a project we've been working on for a while makes us upset.

We think of things in a certain way and they translate into the way we feel. We even anticipate feeling a certain way and yet find ourselves feeling something with more intensity than we expected. It is the frequency and intensity that needs to be tamed. Sometimes even the smallest of comments can trigger us. Happiness transforms into excessive giddiness, frustration into aggression, anger into violence, and disappointment into deep despair. When small things escalate, our mood changes from being content one minute to sad or agitated the next. If you are wondering how to go about this, let's see how our thoughts and emotions shape each other.

THOUGHTS

A mind-boggling fact for you: your brain processes more than 6000 thoughts every single day. It is all the things that you go through during your day, driven by the world around you and the ideas and beliefs that you have formed as you go about your life. If you allow every thought to have an impact on your mood and behavior, you will spend a lifetime reacting instead of getting work done.

Everything that goes through your brain is shaped by many different factors, including where you have been born, what you are taught, and everything that you have experienced. Whether they are positive or negative, all thoughts are based on the perspectives that we bring to any situation. However, thoughts are still within our conscious control. We can learn to be aware of our thoughts, recognize where they come from, and direct them as we see fit.

FIVE TECHNIQUES TO REGULATE YOUR THOUGHTS

1. Identify The Thoughts You Want To Change

It should go without saying that before attempting to manage your thoughts, you must first identify them. Virtually everyone experiences sad thoughts or emotional setbacks occasionally. Intrusive thoughts are also common. That said, negative self-talk or a pessimistic outlook, if occurring regularly, can impact your choices and interactions. The following suggestions that come next can be most effectively used if you can identify particular thoughts and behavior patterns. Sit down with your thoughts and identify the patterns that you would like to alter. It is much tougher to maintain control of your thoughts or your general mood if you are currently going through some difficulties in your life so this is best done when you are not feeling agitated.

2. Accept Unwanted Thoughts

No one likes to be unhappy which is why it makes sense to refrain from thinking about all the negative thinking that happens in our head. Yet ignoring uncomfortable thoughts won't help you regain control. That said, the bigger danger is it might just get worse.

Do the reverse instead: Accept those thoughts. Say you are struggling with making friends at school and even though you have tried to reach out, you are still sitting alone at break time. Accept the scenario. Tell yourself that you are struggling to form connections. It might even offer you clues regarding your personality and behavior. You come to understand that you genuinely want to make connections with your classmates instead of being a lone wolf. This fact alone might encourage you to not settle for things as they are or give up. Once you accept that, it is easier to do step number 3.

3. Change Your Perspective

How we talk to ourselves really matters. One simple technique to change perspective is to talk to yourself in the third person. It might feel a little awkward, but when you put distance between yourself and the situation, you are in a better position to see the bigger picture. Secondly, deliberately deciding to look at things from a third-person perspective helps you to explore your emotions in a better manner.

"I feel awful, but I have gone through terrible things" might give you momentary strength but if you say, "I know you are miserable right now, but you have worked really hard to handle challenges in the past and I am sure you will figure out a way to get through this too" might just give you hope for the future. You can continue the exercise by asking yourself questions in the third person too: "What made [your name] feel this way?"

4. Focus On Positives

The way you view things matters. Putting a positive spin on your woes doesn't mean pretending there's nothing wrong, ignoring problems, or burying your head in the sand.

Rather, it involves looking on the bright side. Every cloud has a silver lining moment. Say you injured your finger during practice and can no longer play in the match. You can blame yourself which will only make you feel worse. Or you can accept the scenario.

You could be grateful you did not get seriously injured or that you will be good to go by the time the next tournament starts. Putting a positive spin will not change the actual outcome of a situation, but it can change the way you feel about your circumstances.

5. Mediation Via Guided Imagery

We keep coming to this one so you know how beneficial mediation can be.

A simple way to enhance your mood and control your thoughts is to try guided imagery. All you have to do is create a relaxing scene in your mind. Think about all the details you associate with the landscape. It could be a bright sunny day, blue skies, or the beach. Once you are there mentally, visualize the details. Think about what time of the day it is. Imagine the sights and smells of the place. Feel the breeze on your face.

It can be any place that brings you peace. Breathe in and out peacefully as you let the scene take over you. Spend 10 to 15 minutes enjoying your image. Now that we have handled the thoughts, let us looks into the emotional side of things.

EMOTIONS AND THEN SOME

Emotions are the inner feelings of a person that come about as a result of their thoughts and behaviors. Some examples of emotions are joy, sadness, fear, guilt, or anger. Every person in the world experiences emotions in the same way – this means that emotions and feelings, whether big or small, positive or negative, are natural and universal, and part of our human experience.

The Connection Between Thoughts And Emotions

As mentioned earlier, emotions are universal. Feelings and emotions are how people across the world connect and bond, over shared joys and sadness. But let's look at a simple scenario: on a summer afternoon, two boys experience something similar – rainfall. One of them is nine years old and lives in England. The other is also nine but lives in the middle of a desert in South America. How do you think each of them will react to what is essentially the same event in each of their lives?

Clearly, many factors affect how we perceive situations, including our history and where we come from. Likewise, thoughts have an influence too - they have a profound effect on your emotions. Most thoughts that we have, even if we don't notice them, trigger feelings in us – Sarah thought she might not do well during her presentation, and that triggered fear and nervousness inside her. She was agitated about the math quiz and unhappy with the world, and the friend's comment unhinged her.

Your thoughts are powerful and can influence your emotions. If you think a dog walking down the street looks friendly and beautiful, you will feel happy to see it. Deem it as a scary creature and you would rather move aside when it crosses you on the sidewalk.

EMOTIONAL REGULATION

Emotional regulation is the ability to understand big feelings and manage our reactions to them, without the emotions spilling over or getting overwhelming. You can imagine a container inside you that holds all your emotions. When the emotions are too big and too intense, the container cannot hold them any longer, and they 'spill over'. The spilling over of emotions is the big, unmanaged reactions that we sometimes have; yelling, for example, or losing control in some way. Self-regulation is about learning to grow this container inside you so it can hold all the emotions.

Emotional regulation is a skill. Like any skill, it takes time and effort to develop, slowly and with practice and patience. It starts when you are a baby and the process can continue well into adulthood.

Four Tips For Emotional Regulation

1. Learn to name the feeling: Frustrated, anxious, terrified, exhausted, and so on. Knowing what you are feeling is the first step towards being able to understand where big feelings are coming from.
2. Tune in to how your body feels: Learn to pause and notice the way your physical reaction to your emotions. Your heartbeat becomes faster, your palms feel sweaty, your face feels flushed, your shoulders slouch, you start fidgeting with your hands, and you tap the leg a little too much. The mind and body have a very strong connection. Sometimes, simply being aware of how we are feeling in a given moment will be enough to help us regulate our reactions to stimuli.
3. Use a calming strategy or a relaxation technique: this could be anything that works for you, from deep breathing to music, movement, sensory activities, or simply taking some alone time to recalibrate.
4. Practice self-care: these are simply the things we do for ourselves that keep us physically and mentally healthy and make us feel happy and energized. These could include anything you like, from playing your favorite sport to having a one-on-one day out with one of your parents, to just making a piece of art or a craft.

Five Reminders About Emotions

1. Accept that thoughts and feelings are connected: At the risk of repeating myself, accepting this connection is the foundation stone of managing your emotions. It all begins with taking charge of your thoughts – if you don't think you'll ever be able to score an A on the math test, the thoughts running through your head will be all about how you hate math, and how you wish this day was already over. That will then cause you to become grumpy, downcast, dejected, and irritated. However, if you just kicked the winning goal for your soccer team, you will naturally be feeling pretty awesome! The thoughts going through your head at that moment will probably be about how happy you are and how amazing everything is about that day!

2. Emotions come and go: Part of acknowledging your emotions is also recognizing that all feelings naturally come and go. Nothing is permanent: you are not angry – you are angry right now. Happy, sad, and angry are not labels – they only indicate a passing emotion. Once you understand this, it will be easier to accept that the feeling will pass.

3. There is no such thing as a 'good' or 'bad' emotion: A lot of times you will hear people around you categorize emotions as 'good' or 'bad' – happy, excited, and hopeful are said to be 'good', and angry,

scared, jealous are supposedly 'bad'. But we can think about these a bit differently – none of these feelings are good or bad. Each of these is a relevant and important passing emotion that helps us make sense of our reality and the world around us and deserves to be felt and understood.

4. Having thoughts about something doesn't make it true: Your thoughts are a product of your brain trying to make sense of reality, and what you have experienced in your life so far. Just because you are experiencing a passing emotion, doesn't mean that it is an indisputable fact.

5. You cannot control how other people think and feel: Even though someone might say 'You make me so angry', their feelings have nothing to do with you, and vice versa. What they think and feel relates to them alone, and they are responsible for how they are feeling.

There is one important fact that you need to tell yourself: thoughts and feelings are controlled by our minds. By learning to recognize our emotions, we can then decide, if we want, to change them by either pulling ourselves out of situations that are causing us to have big, negative feelings or by stepping outside of ourselves and learning to look at the picture from a different angle, maybe a more positive one.

EMPATHY AND COMPASSION

If you have read 'To Kill a Mockingbird', you'll remember something Scott's father says to her, *"You never really understand a person until you consider things from his point of view... until you climb into his skin and walk around in it."*

Scott's father Atticus told her this so she could learn to get along better with all kinds of people. Not everyone thinks in the same way as we do or has the same opinions about something. Empathy is the ability to understand how someone else feels. There are two parts to empathy: sharing a feeling with someone, and by understanding how someone else is seeing something.

The first part is the reason we sometimes feel sad if someone else goes through something, or feel joyful when something good happens to someone we know. The second part is about being able to understand someone else's way of looking at a situation, even if we see things differently; for example, you might enjoy a game that your friend thinks is super boring. You could still like that game while understanding where your friend is coming from – maybe they like less active games, or maybe they just don't enjoy something that makes everyone get so competitive.

Empathy helps us to communicate with the people around us. It helps us understand what someone is trying to say to us and it helps us put across our thoughts and ideas in a way that someone else will understand. It helps us form better relationships, be able to get along with others, and be part of a team.

Compassion is the ability to understand and be kind to someone, even if you don't know exactly what they are going through. Self-compassion is about being kind to yourself, even when you are not able to do something exactly as you wanted to or were expecting. We can sometimes be very hard on ourselves. As teenagers, especially, we go through moments of self-consciousness and self-doubt that cause us to experience feelings of shame and embarrassment. It is important to tell ourselves that everyone goes through failures and setbacks in life. People are not perfect. We also need to learn to talk to ourselves with kindness, the same way we would talk to a friend or someone we care about. You can try the following activity to help yourself through periods of self-doubt and anxiety.

ACTIVITY TIME

Try this activity to practice self-compassion and be able to work through the big feelings that come up in your life. Sit in a quiet room and think of a situation in your life that has been stressful for you. This can be anything that is causing you some discomfort.

When you think of this situation, notice what you are feeling in your body, perhaps discomforts such as tightness in the chest, or a lump in your throat.

Think about the tough moments and tell yourself you are not alone in this. Give yourself a kind, encouraging pat. You may place your hand on your heart. Notice the weight of the hand and how it makes you feel. Geel your heart beating.

Tell yourself that you will be kind to yourself too. If you feel awkward doing this, pretend you are talking to a good friend. Comfort yourself as you would comfort them.

ACTION STEPS

1. Write It Out

Although writing down your thoughts won't necessarily make you feel better right away, it can help you gain more control over unpleasant emotions. Often, just putting things on paper is enough to make it less intense.

2. Practice Following Cues

Try to gauge body language and facial expressions to figure out what someone else is feeling. What does it mean if someone is frowning? What if their arms are crossed? What if someone is rolling their eyes? A great way to understand empathy is to look at the illustrations in picture books. Are there any expressions on the character's faces that reveal how they are feeling?

3. Walk A Mile In Their Shoes

Try to see things from their perspective. Picture this: you made a truly fantastic painting today. You are over the moon, so proud of yourself! But then your dad walks into the room and even though he loves the painting, he doesn't look as happy as you are feeling – is he seeing your accomplishment differently? Look around. Maybe he sees the mess that you made as something that he now has to clean up, so the activity was not as fun for him as it was for you.

4. Develop A Mantra

Think of words you can repeat when you feel overwhelmed. If you are looking to develop one, try using positive affirmations. Here are some ideas:

i. I am grounded
ii. nI am safe
iii. Life is full of joy

5. Destress By Doing The Walking Meditation

Imagine there is a line on the ground. Walk over it, slowly and deliberately (10 to 20 steps is good enough to start). Go slower than you usually would. Put one foot in front of the other and match your breathing to the motion. Notice how the weight of your body shifts. Complete a step fully before beginning the next.

6. Focused Distractions

Doing so deliberately and consciously can help redirect thoughts and improve your mood. This could range from finishing a book you have been reading cleaning your room, spending time with a pet, and so on. Even a nice shower can work as a great way to distract yourself. Just make sure you are using distractions as a temporary break, not complete denial or avoidance.

7. Get Moving

Physical activity is by far the best way to maintain a happy and healthy mind. Exercise releases happy endorphins. Pick a sport or go for a jog and try to incorporate it into your routine. If you cannot manage those, put on a dance routine on youtube and get moving. Don't make it a once-in-a-blue-moon activity. Rather try to do it on a regular basis.

There will come a point when you can effectively control your emotions and reactions. It will be more difficult to self-regulate at other times. Thoughts and feelings become more difficult to grasp when we are ill, exhausted, or over-worked, and we are more likely to behave without thinking. Things can also become too much when our habits or environment change, such as when we switch schools. When this happens, it's crucial to remember what we have learned, be kind to ourselves, and have patience with ourselves. That said, as you learn to be kind to yourself, the next chapter delves into developing and maintaining a kind and respectful relationship with the people we interact with.

8

THE PARENT CONNECTION CAN HELP YOU BE THE PERSON YOU WANT TO BE

C *laire was quiet throughout the car ride. It was my grandma's 75th birthday and there was a big party with extended family and friends. She has always been calm and composed but she loved her Nana and I was expecting a bit more enthusiasm. She had cribbed about going earlier as well but I thought she wasn't too happy about the long car ride out of state.*

As the car stopped and we got off, she literally raced out of the car, with her backpack tightly clutched, and found a seat in the furthest corner of the room. Every time I introduced her to an old neighbor or a distant aunt, she gave me a stare as if I were some Chinese tormentor.

I was a bit bewildered. Was she tired? I looked over my shoulder to check on her and noticed her fidgeting incessantly, tapping her foot rapidly and twirling her hair around her fingers.

A bunch of girls her age were dancing somewhere. Claire watched out of the corner of her eye and I could feel that she wanted to join them but wouldn't. I encouraged her and even offered to go with her but she said she would rather hang out with me, her dad, and Aunt Emily. It was a long night, and she warmed up to a few people by the end. She was quite surprised that she had so many second and third cousins.

Someone called out her name to ask a question. I noticed her freeze for a brief second, then turn red. Her voice quivered before she responded. It was one of those lightbulb moments before it hit me: my daughter wasn't just shy, she was scared.

As I lay in bed that night wondering about this sudden behavior change, I realized something. The two of us hadn't really hung out much socially. It was almost always at home, in our PJs, or a drive from one place to another. Even family dinners were just us and the three kids because we lived far away from family. I had noticed that lately, she preferred being with her friends or staying in her room but I chalked it up to hormones. I wondered how she was at school. None of the teachers had ever complained, save the occasional comment about not being focused or participating in class but she always got good grades. She had a few friends and did hang out with them but we had never reached a point where I told her she had been on the phone long enough or had enough friend time for the week.

Claire had a loving parent who was actively involved and yet she missed the signs. This can be for many different reasons - kids have a different disposition at home and a different persona outside.

Don't beat yourself up for missing the signs, it happens. Parenting is a wholesome experience and that also means your actions on one specific day do not reflect your journey as a parent. As a parent, among other things, one of our jobs is to guide and help the kids find their strengths and overcome their struggles. The following section is specifically geared towards parents and tackles three of the most important areas - effective communication, helping children overcome social struggles, and raising empathetic, kind kids. Here you will find a range of ideas and suggestions that parents can embrace to guide, mentor, and coach their kids as they make the journey to be socially adaptable young adults.

SOCIAL COMPETENCE

One of the first things parents should seek to do is observe their kid in a variety of social settings (e.g., classroom, scout meetings, free play). Claire's mom stumbled on the behavior because she was observant and attuned to the changes in her daughter's demeanor. She did not dismiss the actions or make excuses for herself or her daughter. She paused, reflected, and understood the scenario that had unfolded before making any haphazard judgments.

- Pay attention. The way you communicate sends a message as much as the words you utter. You can make your child feel important by showing concern, making eye contact, and paying attention. Put that phone down, let go of the chores for a brief minute, turn around, and speak to your kid. One other advantage of doing this is, they will not feel the need to act out to get your attention. When they tell you a story about something that happened at school, don't just grumble; pay attention to what they are saying. Kids catch up on these cues from parents and act in similar ways around other people as a result.

- Talk about it. If you notice your child acting poorly, don't ignore it or act as if it did not happen. Instead, choose to speak with them and have a talk about it. When you address it objectively, children see their mistakes, and they are more likely to accept responsibility for it, and eventually alter their behavior.

- But don't lose your temper. Refuse to put up with rude behavior but don't do that by lashing out either. In a sense, you are doing what they are doing - being rude or offensive. If Claire's mom had gotten upset about her not interacting with her family, she would have alienated her daughter. That's not going to solve anything. Take a breath, pause, and communicate the message in a level-headed way.

- Be kind and respectful. Agree to disagree. Give them the information they need and let them form their own opinions. You cannot force them to think a certain way. Instead of trying to convince them, agree to disagree. First of all, parents and kids are two distinct groups of people with unique personalities and worldviews. Every member of the family will foster greater respect and kindness once they come together and embrace their differences. Children who learn to tolerate diversity at home will be more tolerant overall.

- When your child opens up about some social difficulty they have experienced, do not get upset about how they have reacted. They did the best they could and it is your responsibility to equip them. A strong reaction will likely result in them refraining from telling you in the future. Instead, thank them for sharing the experience with you and discuss your options for moving forward.

- As tempting as it may be, teaching your child important skills in times of high stress will not yield any results. Wait for things to settle down before addressing the issue. They will be more receptive when they are calm.

HELPING THEM DECODE NONVERBAL CUES

Is your child struggling to decode the meaning behind their teacher's tight-lipped smiles or his friend's eye rolls? You can use a variety of ways to help your child understand how people communicate without words. Make it engaging by using the following strategies.

- Connect the Message to the Movement

Explain how specific emotions can be portrayed by different body movements. You could try tapping your feet, frowning, and sighing to show frustration. Or you could demonstrate how nervousness shows up as fidgeting, avoiding eye contact, or touching your face again and again.

- Point It Out

Watch real-life interactions and TV shows with your child and highlight non-verbal cues like expressions and gestures. A good way to do this is by switching off the sound on the TV and letting your child focus on the cues. Saying things like "She's shaking her head" or "He's standing with his hands on his hips" helps them remember and interpret the cues that they see.

- Play Body Language Charades

Play charades but with a twist. It may seem like your kids are too old to play these games but there is always that one fun family night that starts with eye rolls and ends with laughter. If you are willing to give it a try, write different emotions on a card (happy, sad, angry, etc) Take turns acting out the emotion while the rest of the group tries to guess it.

- Look at the Bigger Picture

Teach your child that gestures and body movements are just a piece of the puzzle; they need to look at the context and pay attention to the words to get the whole meaning. For instance, a friend could simply be crossing their arms because they're cold, or they could be fidgeting because they're nervous, and not bored.

EMOTIONAL REGULATION

Emotional regulation is the ability to understand big feelings and manage reactions without the emotions spilling over or getting overwhelming. You can imagine a container inside you that holds all your emotions. When the emotions are too big and too intense, the container cannot hold them any longer, and they 'spill over'. The spilling over of emotions is the big, unmanaged reactions that we sometimes have; yelling, for example, or losing control in some way.

1. You are their role model so become one. Work to build up your emotional regulation skills and model these in difficult situations. It is also important to show your kids appropriate responses when they are going through challenging emotions or meltdowns.

2. Do not dismiss emotions. Allow your child or teen to feel and sit with all their emotions, even the tough ones, by acknowledging their feelings and not minimizing, dismissing, or rushing them.

3. Lecture less and listen more. Parents have a lot of experience and they feel it's imperative to share this wealth of information with their children. Unfortunately, lengthy or agitated lectures are ineffective. If you want to engage, avoid asking questions like try: "What's wrong with you?" or "What were you thinking?" A better idea is to ask, "Is there anything I can do to help you feel better?" or "How do you want to go about it?"

4. Don't blame or shame. Nagging, judging, punishing, or yelling will not help. They are learning and they are going to make mistakes. Accept that. It's how they grow in knowledge. When your children come to you for advice, resist the desire to point the finger at them or put them in the negative spotlight. Instead, practice compassion and understanding. Encourage them to reflect on what they have learned from the experience and to process their feelings.

5. Don't let things escalate. There are so many things that happen daily that leave us feeling spent and exhausted. Stumble on a challenging scenario during those moments and there is a greater chance that a conversation with your child would escalate into a heated argument. A simple phrase like "Let's talk about this later. I need some time to think about it" can give you a breather instead of getting riled up.

6. Refrain from using threats. You tell your kids to clean the table and they say something like, "I will do it later". It is very tempting to yell at them or threaten to ground them. Most parents use screen time as a bargaining chip. Unfortnyaltly, most of us don't follow through. In any case, threats don't often work, and end up damaging the relationship. Frustrating, yes but also normal for our kids to push the boundaries. You can be angry but threats will not do much.

7. Help them think things through. Check-in with your kids to see how things are going if you know or suspect that they are having a problem. Encourage them to consider their options. Ask questions that may help them look at the matter from a new angle. Help your child build coping skills. This can be done by helping them face challenges, reflecting on emotions, and expressing them keeping reasonable boundaries in mind.

There will come a point when you can effectively control your emotions and reactions. It will be more difficult to self-regulate at other times. Thoughts and feelings become more difficult to grasp when we are ill, exhausted, or over-worked, and we are more likely to behave without thinking. Things can also become too much when our habits or environment change, such as when we switch jobs or move to a new house. Life changes like an unwell relative, divorce, financial insecurity, or a fight with the spouse can affect our mood and reaction. When this happens, it's crucial to remember what we've learned, be kind to ourselves, and have patience with ourselves.

TEAMWORK

All of us want our kids to be successful. That's why we go the extra mile to give them the best education and opportunities. But sometimes we overlook the fact that success is not limited to individual achievement; our ability to work well in a team is a crucial skill for being successful. Whether your kids are tackling a science fair project or a soccer game, they'll need to be a team player to make it happen.

Not everyone is a born team player; many kids are too shy or too bossy and struggle with teamwork skills. Some are solo performers in a group setting. Teamwork may make the dream work, but for some kids, it's a nightmare. Thankfully, parents can provide valuable support and guidance. Help your child become a team player. You can following activities to strengthen that team spirit:

- Enroll your child in a league sport, such as football, dance, or Scouts. In addition to having fun, kids get to interact with other kids who share their interests. Everyone benefits from it.
- Do some team-building games to get things going. Games like Jenga, Charades, Egg-Drop, and Scrabble are excellent for teaching teamwork and taking turns.
- Show your family how great it is to operate as a team. Ask everyone to help out with the tasks, and don't forget to recognize those who do the most, or do so without being prompted.

ACTION STEPS

1. Empathise And Stay Real

Rather than using "you" statements, try using "I" statements that focus on how you feel. "You" statements can put your kids on the defensive right away. Instead of "You did not study for the exam" try saying "I am worried that you won't do as well as you expect on the exam".

2. Make It Easy For Them To Engage With You

Teens/preteens can find it difficult to open up to people about what is going on in their lives because they are afraid of being judged.

It's critical to maintain open lines of communication, especially during the formative adolescent years. Some simple ways to keep the lines of communication open are:

- Giving them choices so they feel in control
- Listening more and criticizing less
- Asking them about their interests and pastimes
- Open-ended questions that allow them to speak
- Not interrupting or swooshing your expert opinion right away
- Using simple but powerful phrases like "Tell me more."

3. Be Nice

Find ways and excuses to be nice. Say positive things to them every day. If you notice them being respectful or kind, mention it in conversation. Physical connection is equally important. You do not have to hug all the time. A gentle pat on the shoulder can do the job. Fist bumps, high fives, and even a wink or a smile as you pass them in the kitchen is a feel-good gesture.

4. Strengthen The Bond

Do things together. You can run errands together, go grocery shopping, and watch a movie or a game. Additionally, actively engage in a long-term activity. Some ideas are:

- Plan and budget for a special purchase
- Gardening
- Long-term crafts like repainting an old dresser or making a swing together
- Do large puzzles

5. Pinpoint The Problem

Don't generalize about what you think your child is or isn't doing. If you see them using their phone relentlessly even though there is an assignment, talking about the assignment instead of phone usage. The issue is poor time management and that is what needs to be highlighted. Your kids will be less likely to become defensive when you focus on particular behaviors instead of throwing blanket statements.

6. Remove Barriers To Communication

This can be anything. Some kids don't like talking in front of their siblings or the other parent. Some prefer having conversations in the car because it takes away the pressure of face-to-face conversation. Understand the needs and preferences of your kids to improve your chances of being heard. Give them complete attention without passing judgment, and refrain from offering unasked-for advice unless they specifically ask for it.

7. Focus On Action Not Result

Don't force your children to interact in big groups if you know they struggle with it. Start small, and provide activities that give them lots of chances to do so. Expand the circle gradually. Moreover, do not compare. Do not focus on winning or losing. Instead, emphasize and encourage them for their involvement, enjoyment, contribution, and satisfaction in challenging activities.

You understand the importance of communicating, teamwork, emotional regulation, and social engagement but, your teen/preteen may not. You cannot force them to embrace your opinions but you can teach them these skills so they learn them over time. There are times when your little ones aren't comfortable talking to you about routine issues, much less challenging ones. Learning how to communicate is essential to maintaining a healthy relationship and that requires hard work, like everything else in life. It requires effort and commitment. If you want to build connections, being gentle and kind is the only way to go forward. It will surely take a lot of effort and commitment on your part but it's worthwhile. Even if you pick three things from this section, you will notice positive changes in your relationship. The key is to start because once you do, you won't be able to stop yourself!

HOW IT ALL STARTED

As we reach the last leg of our little journey, let's talk about Lisa's journey and why she inspired me to write this book.

Lisa entered the workforce as an entry-level information analyst in a top-notch organization a little after she graduated. It came as a surprise because she wasn't someone who particularly enjoyed crunching data. We convinced her because it would look good on her resume and the money was good.

I don't know if I would call it the best thing to happen to her or the worst. Things started to change soon after she joined. Her replies were evasive but measured. She was always stressed. Worried. Agitated. I asked her many times only to be told off. It was around Christmas and we were set up to meet some old friends but Lisa refused to leave the house. She said she had come home so she doesn't have to meet anyone. She had to be coaxed to step out of the house when she was younger but I thought things had changed by now. I told her to grow and up and then the crying started. My grown-up adult child was crying. Amidst the tears and the sobs, she talked about the things bogging her down. She talked about work, or rather, how much she hated being at work. How she spent her days praying she wouldn't have to present. She explained all those random phone calls to me because that was her pretending to be on the phone so she wouldn't have to sit with colleagues. It was just like her going to the library in school. She felt like she did not belong in her new world and this was draining her emotionally.

She talked about how she had started doubting every word that came out of her mouth, how she read and reread every email she sent. She recounted story after story about avoiding the coffee station if her colleagues were gathered around it. Everyone would be chatting casually while she rehearsed answers in her head.

I tried to recall her carefree life only to remember that she had always been this way. She wasn't a talker and definitely not someone with many friends. She had dodged the problem in my younger years but her incapacity to ask questions in class evolved into an unwillingness to do so at crucial meetings which meant she couldn't do her job properly.

What was fine back then, wasn't going to work in the professional world. Her social anxiety was holding her back in her career. She was ok with it in school but it hurt to see everyone around her advancing in their career while she was getting overlooked.

It was a long night and an even longer week. I saw her return to work with her head down and it hurt me so much. Something had to change. We had two choices. Continue to sit in the corner, make notes and keep her head down, or take control of social anxiety. Lisa and I chose the latter. I did not know what that meant but if we wanted to stop feeling this way, we had to make some hard calls.

We looked around for examples but only found well-functioning adults who had it all figured out (or so it seemed to me). Lisa turned to the internet, her forever companion in life. She read up on the experiences of other people who struggled with similar challenges. Turns out, she was not alone. The world is filled with people with anxiety, the kind who felt awkward, embarrassed, and downright incompetent every time they stepped out of the house.

According to The National Institute Of Mental Health, social anxiety disorder (SAD) Over 19 million people across America suffer from social anxiety. Worth mentioning here is that it is quite intense in teenagers as well. It affects 1 out of 3 adolescents between 13 and 18 years old. It is the most common anxiety disorder and the third most common mental health disorder in the country.

Knowing she wasn't the odd one out made Lisa feel better. All those people she always thought had it all figured out were probably struggling too. They had just figured out how to manage their anxiety. If they could do that, why couldn't she?

It also made it easier for me to accept that there was a problem. That my daughter had a social phobia. We had always told ourselves that she was just an introvert who enjoyed staying at home.

I saw Lisa devise an action plan. She took baby steps. She made little changes every few days. She read dozens of websites and books. She attended motivational talks and looked up Ted Talks on YouTube. She would come home and write it all down. The journals that we filled over the years helped her come out of that dark place. And in this book, I am compiling all that information so you don't have to look around.

As I mentioned at the start of this book, the things I learned have allowed me to view things in a different light. My daughter endured life in high school, and beyond for years. She struggled and I did not see the clues too well. I have taken time to come to terms with it but now that I am equipped with the knowledge, I don't want to limit my experiences to myself. I am putting it all here so you can use our experiences, struggles, and weak moments, to make those changes now. Just do some exercises. Turn the page, pick an action step, and take that first step.

Let's stop falling back on our tried and tested safety behaviors. Simba spent years in isolation but only found peace when he confronted his fears and returned home. Life is to be lived, not endured. Be your own superhero, be your own rock star. Lisa found the light because she dared to enter. So will you. Surely you have the power. Close your eyes, and take that step.

HELLO, AND THANK YOU FOR PURCHASING MY BOOK!

Many readers are unaware of what a difference even one review makes.

I would greatly appreciate it if you could help other teens and parents of teens struggling with social skills find my book on Amazon by leaving a review.

It only takes 3 minutes, and I have made it easy for you to help!
Just click on the link below or scan the QR code with your phone.
I am very grateful for your support.

https://amzn.to/3QYxkqM

REFERENCES

6 Tips for Teaching Your Children Teamwork | Macaroni KID National. (n.d.). Macaroni KID National. https://national.macaronikid.com/articles/ 59a70aaa6a33644cae651292/6-tips-for-teaching-your-children- teamwork

10 Important Social Skills You Need to Teach Your Teen Now. (n.d.). Raising Teens Today.

10 Tips to Take Charge of Your Mindset and Control Your Thoughts. (2021, January 8). Healthline. https://www.healthline.com/health/mental- health/how-to-control-your-mind#naming

13 Ways on How to Help Your Teen Make Friends. (2022, December 27). Ashley Hudson LMFT. https://www.ashleyhudsontherapy.com/post/ 13-ways-on-how-to-help-your-teen-make-friends

22 Body Language and Facial Expressions And What They Show: Find New Ways Of Communication | BetterHelp. (n.d.). https://www.betterhelp. com/advice/body-language/22-body-language-examples-and-what- they-show/

A lot of problems in the world would disappear if we talked to each other instead of about each other. - Tiny Buddha. (2016, May 18). Tiny Buddha. https://tinybuddha.com/wisdom-quotes/lot-problems-world-disap pear-talked-instead/

A Moment for Me: A Self-Compassion Break for Teens | Greater Good In Education. (2022, January 6). Greater Good in Education. https://ggie. berkeley.edu/practice/a-moment-for-me-a-self-compassion-break- for-teens/

Admin. (2019). How To Teach Your Child To Be Kind And Respectful. *Winmore.* https://www.winmoreacademy.com/how-to-teach-your- child-to-be-kind-and-respectful/

Anxiety and Difficulty Speaking. (2022, September 6). www.calmclinic.com. https://www.calmclinic.com/anxiety/symptoms/difficulty-speaking

Any Anxiety Disorder. (n.d.). National Institute of Mental Health (NIMH). https://www.nimh.nih.gov/health/statistics/any-anxiety-disorder

BA, V. S. B. (2022, July 9). *11 Signs Someone Doesn't Want To Be Your Friend.* SocialSelf. https://socialself.com/blog/signs-not-friends/

BBC. (2017). 6 major stars who prefer life as an introvert. *BBC.* https://www.bbc.co.uk/programmes/articles/2ykqrq7PRDZ9YVmNxBZbR8y/6-major-stars-who-prefer-life-as-an-introvert

Begin Learning Team. (2023, May 16). *Teaching Feelings: 7 Ways To Help Kids Understand Their Emotions - Begin Learning.* Begin Learning. https://www.learnwithhomer.com/homer-blog/4133/teaching-feelings/

BoruchAkbosh. (2019). Developing Critical Thinking Skills of a Teenager. *Risepreneur.* https://www.risepreneur.com/developing-critical-thinking-skills-of-a-teenager/

Bryant, C. D. (n.d.). *What are Social Skills? Definition of social skills for kids.* Talking With Trees Books. https://talkingtreebooks.com/teaching-resources-catalog/definitions/what-are-social-skills.html

Burstein, M., Ameli-Grillon, L., & Merikangas, K. R. (2011). Shyness Versus Social Phobia in US Youth. *Pediatrics, 128*(5), 917–925. https://doi.org/10.1542/peds.2011-1434

10 Steps To Overcome Social Anxiety 2011-2023. (n.d.). *Beat Social Anxiety, Build Confidence | SkillsYouNeed.* https://www.skillsyouneed.com/rhubarb/overcome-social-anxiety.html

Carducci, B. J. (n.d.). Everything you ever wanted to know about shyness in an international context. *https://www.apa.org.* https://www.apa.org/international/pi/2017/06/shyness

Carlton, T. (2020). Social Skills: A Learned Behavior. *Blue Bird Day.* https://bluebirddayprogram.com/social-skills-a-learned-behavior/

Causes Of Social Awkwardness | www.succeedsocially.com. (n.d.). https://www.succeedsocially.com/relatedfactors

Cherry, K. (2022). How to Start a Conversation. *Verywell Mind.* https://www.verywellmind.com/how-to-start-a-conversation-4582339#toc-prepare-ahead-of-time

Colleen, S. (2020, October). *Shyness.* Nemours Teen Health.

Corinne. (2020). 8 Highly Effective Ways for Teaching Kids Respect & How to Be Polite. *The Pragmatic Parent.* https://www.thepragmaticparent.com/teaching-kids-respect/

Council, Y. E. (2021, January 5). Master the Art of Small Talk in 7 Steps.

Inc.com. https://www.inc.com/young-entrepreneur-council/master-art-of-small-talk-in-7-steps.html

Cuncic, A. (2020). A Day in the Life of a Teenager With Social Anxiety Disorder. *Verywell Mind.* https://www.verywellmind.com/social-anxiety-disorder-teenager-3024738

"Dos and Don'ts" for Fostering Social Competence. (n.d.). LD OnLine. https://www.ldonline.org/ld-topics/behavior-social-skills/dos-and-donts-fostering-social-competence

Dwyer-Jones, S. (2021). 7 Celebrities You Did not know had anxiety. *Healthista.* https://www.healthista.com/5-celebrities-you-didnt-know-had-anxiety-2/

Edsys. (2019, July 30). 17 Best Confidence Building Activities and Games For Youngsters. *Edsys.* https://www.edsys.in/best-confidence-building-activities-and-games/

Elkind, D. (1994). *Parenting Your Teenager.*

Emotional Regulation: Skills, Exercises, and Strategies. (n.d.). https://www.betterup.com/blog/emotional-regulation-skills

Empathy And Understanding Others - Improve Your Social Skills. (2014, April 10). Improve Your Social Skills. https://www.improveyoursocialskills.com/empathy

Engler, B. (2023). Teaching Your Child to Deal with Conflict. *www.connectionsacademy.com.* https://www.connectionsacademy.com/support/resources/article/building-conflict-resolution-skills-in-children/

Era, Y. (2021). How To Use Skills To Logically Solve a Problem. *Youth Empowerment.* https://youthempowerment.com/problem-solving/

'Frenemies' and toxic friendships: pre-teens and teenagers. (2021, September 13). Raising Children Network. https://raisingchildren.net.au/pre-teens/behaviour/peers-friends-trends/frenemies

Friendship Skills - Teenage Resource. (n.d.). Teenage Resource. https://teenage-resource.middletownautism.com/teenage-issues-and-strate gies/social-skills-friendships/friendship-skills/

Friendships and teenagers - ReachOut Parents. (n.d.). https://parents.au.reachout.com/skills-to-build/wellbeing/friendships-and-teenagers

Fry, S. M. (2020). 7 do's and don'ts to help your family build empathy skills. *Parenting.* https://www.greatschools.org/gk/articles/7-dos-and-donts-to-help-your-family-build-eempathy-skills/

Garey, J., PsyD, S. a. L., & Lcsw, C. W. (2023). Teaching Kids How to Deal With Conflict. *Child Mind Institute*. https://childmind.org/article/teaching-kids-how-to-deal-with-conflict/

Ginsburg, K. (2021). 7 Expert Tips for Talking with Teens. *Center for Parent and Teen Communication*. https://parentandteen.com/keep-teens-talking-learn-to-listen/

Gosset, K. (2018, April 19). *Diary of a socially anxious teen*. Stuff. https://www.stuff.co.nz/life-style/parenting/big-kids/tweens-to-teens/103246314/diary-of-a-socially-anxious-teen

Group Dynamix. (2023). How Teamwork Helps Kids Succeed In Life. *Group Dynamix*. https://groupdynamix.com/how-teamwork-helps-kids-succeed-in-life/

Gwen. (2019). Critical Thinking: 11 Problem-Solving Activities for Kids. *Meraki Lane*. https://www.merakilane.com/critical-thinking-11-problem-solving-activities-for-kids/

Harvey-Jenner, C. (2019, March 7). How Taylor Swift manages her anxiety. *Cosmopolitan*. https://www.cosmopolitan.com/uk/body/a26746717/taylor-swift-anxiety-l-theanine/

HealthDay News. (2022, May 30). Shyness, Ages 12 to 16. *Consumer Health News | HealthDay*. https://consumer.healthday.com/encyclopedia/children-s-health-10/child-development-news-124/shyness-ages-12-to-16-645926.html

How ADHD May Be Impacting Your Child's Social Skills and What You Can Do To Help. (n.d.). Foothills Academy. https://www.foothillsacademy.org/community/articles/adhd-social-skills

How I Overcame Social Anxiety: Dave | Social Anxiety Institute. (n.d.). https://socialanxietyinstitute.org/dave-how-i-overcame-social-anxiety

How Low Self-Esteem Can Affect Your Social Life | HealthyPlace. (2019, April 3). https://www.healthyplace.com/blogs/buildingselfesteem/2019/4/how-low-self-esteem-can-affect-your-social-life

How to communicate effectively with your young child. (n.d.). UNICEF Parenting. https://www.unicef.org/parenting/child-care/9-tips-for-better-communication

How To Develop Your Child's Collaboration Soft Skill. (n.d.). Icodeschool.

How To Help Your Older Teenager With Their Social Awkwardness | www.suc-

ceedsocially.com. (n.d.). https://www.succeedsocially.com/helpolderteenager

How To Improve Social Skills in Teens. (n.d.). https://www.bgca.org/news-stories/2022/September/how-to-improve-social-skills-in-teens

How to teach your child teamwork. (n.d.). TheSchoolRun. https://www.theschoolrun.com/how-teach-your-child-teamwork

How to Use the FORD Method in Conversations. (2019, January 10). Our Everyday Life. https://oureverydaylife.com/use-ford-method-conversations-2087525.html

Instagram. (n.d.). https://www.instagram.com/dr.siggie/?hl=en

Kaplan, Z. (2023). What Are Collaboration Skills? Definition and Examples. *Forage.* https://www.theforage.com/blog/skills/collaboration-skills

Kelly, J. (2021, January 4). *"Alone We Can Do So Little; Together We Can Do So Much." Helen Keller - Nimble Quotes.* Nimble Quotes. https://nimblequotes.com/alone-we-can-do-so-little-together-we-can-do-so-much-helen-keller/

Kelly, K. (2023). How to Help Your Child Understand Body Language | Understood. *Understood.* https://www.understood.org/en/articles/at-a-glance-helping-your-child-understand-body-language

Kuzmeski, M. (2019). Small Talk Made Simple: Five Ways to Help Your Kids Feel Comfortable Connecting. *MetroFamily Magazine.* https://www.metrofamilymagazine.com/small-talk-made-simple-five-ways-to-help-your-kids-feel-comfortable-connecting/

Larsen, E. F. (2021, April 30). 10 Ways to Raise a Compassionate Child, According to Experts. *Parents.* https://www.parents.com/parenting/better-parenting/advice/13-ways-to-raise-a-compassionate-child-online-and-off/

Lcsw, A. M. (2021). How to Teach Kids Problem-Solving Skills. *Verywell Family.* https://www.verywellfamily.com/teach-kids-problem-solving-skills-1095015

Leahy, M. (2020, February 5). Our 15-year-old daughter is mostly friendless. Should we help her? *Washington Post.* https://www.washingtonpost.com/lifestyle/on-parenting/our-15-year-old-daughter-is-mostly-friendless-should-we-help-her/2020/02/04/d751dd6e-4374-11ea-b5fc-eefa848cde99_story.html

LMFT, N. a. M. (2021, July 22). *How to Use the F.O.R.D Method (With Example Questions)*. SocialSelf. https://socialself.com/blog/ford-method/

Maltoni, V. (n.d.). *Why is Conversation Important?* Conversation Agent - Valeria Maltoni. https://www.conversationagent.com/2015/10/why-conversation-matters.html

Mightier, E. S. L. a. L. C. S. A. (2023). 5 Emotional Self-Regulation Skills for Kids. *Mightier.* https://www.mightier.com/resources/5-emotional-self-regulation-skills-for-kids/

Mighty. (2017, February 4). A Day in the Life of a Student With an Anxiety Disorder. *Teen Vogue.* https://www.teenvogue.com/story/a-day-in-the-life-of-a-student-with-an-anxiety-disorder

MindTools | Home. (n.d.). https://www.mindtools.com/az4wxv7/active-listening

Monke, A. (2023). 10 Friendship Skills Every Kid Needs. *Sunshine Parenting.* https://sunshine-parenting.com/10-friendship-skills-every-kid-needs/

My Lifelong Struggle With Social Anxiety. (n.d.). Anxiety and Depression Association of America, ADAA. https://adaa.org/living-with-anxiety/personal-stories/my-lifelong-struggle-social-anxiety

Mydoh. (2023). How to Teach Kids Negotiation Skills. *Mydoh.* https://www.mydoh.ca/learn/blog/lifestyle/how-to-teach-your-kids-negotiation-skills

Nikki. (2016, February 29). Social Skills: A Learned Behavior Or Not? *Child's Play Therapy Center.* https://www.childsplaytherapycenter.com/social-skills-is-it-a-learned-behavior-or-not/

Ong, J., & Ong, J. (2021). The Causes of Poor Social Skills | Jason Ong. *Ong Jason.* https://ongjason.com/the-causes-of-poor-social-skills/

Poor Social Skills May Be Harmful to Mental and Physical Health. (2020, July 17). The University of Arizona News. https://news.arizona.edu/story/poor-social-skills-may-be-harmful-mental-and-physical-health

Problem-solving and teenagers - ReachOut Parents. (n.d.). https://parents.au.reachout.com/skills-to-build/connecting-and-communicating/problem-solving-and-teenagers

Rodrigo, G. (2018). Why Kids Should Develop Collaboration As A Life Skill. *Fun Academy.* https://funacademy.fi/collaboration-as-a-life-skill/

Russell, L. (2023). Friendship Skills for Children and Teenagers. *They Are the Future.* https://www.theyarethefuture.co.uk/friendship-skills-chil dren-teenagers/

School, S. P. C. (n.d.). *Teaching teens about respectful language.* St Paul's Collegiate School - Hamilton. https://hail.to/st-pauls-collegiate-school-hamilton/article/7zSr6hk

Scully, S. (2022, April 8). What Is Active Listening? Psychology Experts Share 5 Steps to Enhance Your Communication Skills. *Good Housekeeping.* https://www.goodhousekeeping.com/health/wellness/ a39601657/what-is-active-listening/

Self-compassion for pre-teens and teenagers. (2021, June 9). Raising Children Network. https://raisingchildren.net.au/teens/mental-health-physi cal-health/about-mental-health/self-compassion-teenagers

Self-regulation in children and teenagers. (2021, May 20). Raising Children Network. https://raisingchildren.net.au/toddlers/behaviour/under standing-behaviour/self-regulation

Shameer, M. (2023, April 6). *7 Useful Tips To Help Your Teens Solve Their Problems.* MomJunction. https://www.momjunction.com/articles/ help-your-teen-solve-her-problems_00326769/

Sichterman, J. (2015). Teaching your Child the Art of Negotiation. *Embracing Horizons.* https://embracinghorizons.com/teaching-your-child-the-art-of-negotiation/

Smith, M., MA. (2023a). Anxiety in Children and Teens: A Parent’s Guide. *HelpGuide.org.* https://www.helpguide.org/ articles/anxiety/anxiety-in-children-and-teens.htm

Smith, M., MA. (2023b). Nonverbal Communication and Body Language. *HelpGuide.org.* https://www.helpguide.org/articles/relationships-communication/nonverbal-communication.htm

Social and Teamwork Skills for Children | University of Nevada, Reno. (2022, July 9). University of Nevada, Reno. https://onlinedegrees.unr.edu/ online-master-of-social-work/tips-to-improve-your-childs-social-and-teamwork-skills/

Social anxiety (social phobia). (n.d.). NHS. https://www.nhs.uk/mental-health/conditions/social-anxiety/

Social Skills Assessment - Adolescent. (n.d.). [Slide show]. CSC Family.

http://cscfamily.cscbroward.org/ExternalDownloads/
MOST2006SSAAdolescent.pdf

Social Skills Checklist (Secondary). (n.d.). Success for Kids With Hearing
Loss. https://successforkidswithhearingloss.com/wp-content/
uploads/2011/08/SOCIAL-SKILLS-CHECKLIST-SECONDARY.pdf

Sparks, S. D. (2021, May 3). Children Must Be Taught to Collaborate,
Studies Say. *Education Week.* https://www.edweek.org/leadership/chil
dren-must-be-taught-to-collaborate-studies-say/2017/05

Staff, S. P. (n.d.-a). *13 Ways to Raise a Caring and Compassionate Child.*
https://www.scholastic.com/parents/family-life/social-emotional-
learning/social-skills-for-kids/13-ways-to-raise-caring-and-compas
sionate-child.html

Staff, S. P. (n.d.-b). *How Your Child Learns to Problem-Solve.* https://www.
scholastic.com/parents/family-life/creativity-and-critical-thinking/
learning-skills-for-kids/how-your-child-learns-to-problem-
solve.html

Staff, S. P. (n.d.-c). *How Your Child Learns to Problem-Solve.* https://www.
scholastic.com/parents/family-life/creativity-and-critical-thinking/
learning-skills-for-kids/how-your-child-learns-to-problem-
solve.html

Student Pocket Guide. (2017, July 4). *Why Talking Is Important.* Student
Pocket Guide | UK Student Magazine. https://www.thestudentpocket
guide.com/2017/07/student-life/health-and-relationships/why-talk
ing-is-important/

Svitorka, T. (2022, July 10). 6 Tips How To Master Small Talk And Never
Feel Awkward Again. *Tomas Svitorka - London Life Coach.* https://
tomassvitorka.com/master-small-talk/

Swift struggles to make friends. (2010, May 3). Swift struggles to make
friends. *Irish Examiner.* https://www.irishexaminer.com/lifestyle/
arid-30456177.html

Synapse. (2021, November 25). *Social Skills and Confidence - Synapse.*
https://synapse.org.au/fact-sheet/social-skills-and-confidence/

Team, B. A. S. (2023, April 21). How to Use Meditation for Teen Stress
and Anxiety. *Cleveland Clinic.* https://health.clevelandclinic.org/how-
to-use-meditation-for-teen-stress-and-anxiety/

Team, U. (2023). Trouble With Social Skills | Understood. *Understood.* https://www.understood.org/en/articles/trouble-with-social-skills

Teamwork Skills: Being an Effective Group Member | Centre for Teaching Excellence. (n.d.). https://uwaterloo.ca/centre-for-teaching-excellence/ catalogs/tip-sheets/teamwork-skills-being-effective-group-member#:

TherapyWorks. (2023, March 15). *Teen Social Skills | TherapyWorks.* TherapyWorks | Changing Lives. https://mytherapyworks.com/teen-social-skills

Uk, Y. E. (2020). Communication skills: Ask open-ended questions! Here’s why. *Youth Employment UK.* https://www.youthemploy ment.org.uk/communication-skills-open-ended-questions/

United We Care. (2023). What Causes Lack Of Social Skills In Kids? *United We Care | a Super App for Mental Wellness.* https://www.united wecare.com/what-causes-lack-of-social-skills-in-kids/

Team, G. (2023). Overcome Social Anxiety - Social Anxiety Therapy — Alena. *Alena.* https://alena.com/learn/how-i-overcame-social-anxiety

Ward, A. (2022). 7 Targeted Active Listening Games, Exercises, and Activities for Adults. *The GLS Project.* https://www.goodlisten ingskills.org/active-listening-games-exercises-activities/

What Are Thoughts & Emotions? | Taking Charge of Your Health & Wellbeing. (n.d.). Taking Charge of Your Health & Wellbeing. https://www. takingcharge.csh.umn.edu/what-are-thoughts-emotions

Whyte, A. (2021, January 4). *Should Parents Push a Shy Teen to Be More Social?* Evolve Treatment Centers. https://evolvetreatment.com/blog/ push-shy-teen-social/

Wong, D. (2023). How to Communicate With Teenagers (11 Actionable Tips for Parents). *Daniel Wong.* https://www.daniel-wong.com/2022/ 06/14/communicating-with-teens/

Woods, M. (2022). Conflict Resolution for Teens: 9 Essential Skills » TeenWire.org. *TeenWire.org.* https://www.teenwire.org/ conflict-resolution-for-teens/

Zetlin, M. (2021, January 5). 11 Graceful Ways to End a Conversation That Work 100 Percent of the Time. *Inc.com.* https://www.inc.com/ minda-zetlin/11-foolproof-ways-to-nicely-end-a-conversation.html

Made in United States
Troutdale, OR
10/24/2024

24106896R00100